Don de Santos (Adventure)

Razelle Baldwin

Contents

Chapter 01 - Hermano

It is 3 AM.

The nightmares of the events of last year still haunt me to this day. Ever since my father was captured by the police because of his brother, Ricardo, I have been eating myself alive. My father went to prison because he was blackmailed about something related to me and I can't forgive myself for what happened. I will do anything to break him free, just as I had promised him.

I remove myself from the girl's arm, whose name I don't remember, and left the room to get some water. This happens every day. I have nightmares, get up, get some water, and go back to sleep. I have been living like this for a year.

My men and I devised so many plans to break my father out of the Central Prison of Vancouver, but it is harder than we thought. We needed to know men on the inside who knew about the plan to help my father and that's exactly what we did. Some of my most trusted men, Cash and Alex, volunteered to do an offense and go to jail to be with my father. We wrote a plan that took months to complete to make sure nothing goes wrong. They have been in prison for a month and three days, one for killing a police officer who was harassing a woman, and the other for robbing a bank and distributing the money to the public.

I will forever be indebted to them.

Cash is my right-hand man, while Alex, who's Cash's brother, is the best hacker my mafia has worked with. Cash and Alex were abandoned by their family at the age of ten and thirteen. Their family didn't want them because they couldn't take care of them anymore. I remember Alex once told me that they had more siblings, but they were the ones that their family decided to let go of. If I hadn't found them in that ally, they would have been dead now.

I open the silver fridge, the light of the fridge helped me see around the kitchen as I didn't turn on the lights. I grab a bottle of water and drink it in one go. I panted when I finished, feeling satisfied.

I throw the bottle in the bin and walk back to my room.

The girl is still sleeping and I wanted more than anything to kick her out and have the whole bed to myself. But I am a gentleman, I wouldn't let her drive in the middle of the night alone.

I create some space between me and her and close my eyes, hoping no nightmares interrupt me this time.

2 PM - De Santos Mansion

"Se paciente, Alba!" I hear my mother yell at my sister.

-Be patient

I walk into the kitchen only to see them face to face, ready to get into an argument. My mother and sister love each other a lot, but they shouldn't be put in the same place for more than two hours because one, both of them are bossy, and second, both of them are stubborn.

"Que esta pacando?" I ask, standing between the two, making sure they don't do anything stupid.

-What's going on?

"She wants to cook!" my mother exclaims, pointing at Alba's chest with her index finger.

"So? This is my kitchen too!" Alba replies, her hands flying in the air.

"This is my house!"

"Then I should get a house of my own!" Alba yelled, stomping out of the kitchen like a child.

"Mom, why are you not letting her do anything?" I ask gently.

She sighs and shakes her head. "She's my daughter, I want to cook for her."

I chuckle, pulling her to my chest and hugging her.

That's Victoria Santos, the best mother in the whole world. A little bit controlling, but in a good way. She just wants to see her kids happy. Alba and I are very lucky to have a mother like her. She's sweet, kind, and understanding...well, not always.

"I know, mom, but she's a big girl, and sometimes, she wants to do things alone."

"I know...I'll go and fix it with her," she says, patting my shoulder. "Any news about your father?"

"Not yet, but I am waiting for a call soon from Cash and Alex."

"Oh, those two boys, I have missed them."

"Me too." I grin.

"I'll go check on that troublemaker," my mom says, walking out and leaving me alone in the kitchen.

It is at times like these that I feel somewhat complete, only if my father is here, I'd feel better. He was and still is the don of the Spanish mafia. I only took over when he went to prison, but I can't wait to have him back and work with me.

Ten minutes later, Alba walks into the kitchen again with a huge grin on her face.

"You called it a truce?" I ask and she nods.

I stand up and walk towards her. "Alba, no le vuelvas a gritar asi a mama, de acuerdo?" I gently say, knowing very well that she didn't mean to do it.

-Don't yell at mom like that again, okay?

"Si, Hermano." She nods with a smile.

-Yes, brother.

"So, how's Cash and Alex?" Alba asks as she starts preparing lunch.

"I don't know. Haven't heard from them since they went in."

"How do you know that they are still alive?" she asked.

"Don't worry, they are."

"Can we get them out, already? I miss dad," she says, putting the chopped carrots into the pan.

"Soon, Hermana. Soon. I am supposed to receive a call from them today. If everything goes smoothly, we will break them out in a week."

"I can't wait." She smiles.

"Do you need any help, mi rosa?" I ask.

"Aww, the big, bad mafia don wants to help his sister with cooking?"

"Never mind, you're fine cooking alone," I said, sending her a playful glare, and leaving the kitchen.

I leave my family's house and make my way to the warehouse. Our warehouse is one hour away from the family house. My father wanted to make sure that mom and Alba are away from everything. He made sure no one knew where the mansion is, only family members and trusted men knew.

Halfway, I receive an unknown call. I immediately know that it is the number of the burner phone one of my men gave Cash when he visited him in prison. He was so clever in delivering the phone, without anyone seeing or sensing.

"Hello?"

"Brother," Cash said.

"Good to hear from you, mi Hermano."

"Same here, brother. I don't have much time, but I called to let you know that everything is going according to our plan. They put Alex and me in the same cell since we were caught on the same day. Our cell is three cells away from Don Manuel. He is okay and knows about the plan."

"Hang in there, brother. In a week, you will be out. Take care and tell my father I miss him."

"Will do, see you."

With that, hope made its way back into my heart and for the first time in the past year, I smile.

I am not going to tell my mother anything, just because I don't want to get her hopes up if something goes wrong.

Hopefully, nothing goes wrong.

Chapter 02 - Segunda Hija

It is on days like these that I regret quitting my job at the hospital, but then again, I wasn't going to be able to continue my practice there...not only because I was not allowed, but also because I couldn't.

A man sits in front of me with the guard standing behind him, making sure he doesn't do anything. His name is George and I hate his guts. He is so rude and disrespectful. The first time he saw me, he couldn't but comment on my body.

Pervert.

I give him the monthly shot he takes and sends him on his way. George is one of the reasons I hate coming here, but when

I look back at all the patients I befriended, I feel happy and grateful.

I never had a family that really supported me. My parents only care about their image and money, while my brother, Andrew, and my sister, Sarah, live their own lives just like I am doing. I don't really blame them for not reaching out to me and supporting my decision to work at the prison because I know what it's like to have parents like ours.

I walk back to my desk when another guard walks in. "Dr. Wright, I have prisoner number 581. He says he's in pain."

"Okay, send him in quickly," I reply with furrowed eyebrows.

Prisoner number 581 is Manuel Santos. He is one of the people that I befriended in prison. I am close to him enough to know that he is a good person. I still don't know what he did and I never asked him. What could he have done worst than my crime that no one knew about?

The guard enters again, but this time, with Mr. Santos.

"You can leave," I tell the guard.

"Ma'am, I am not allowed to leave you alone with him," the guard replies, making my blood boil.

"I think you're new here, this is my office and I decide who stays and who leaves," I say harshly, glaring at him.

He hesitantly nods and leaves the room.

"That was a little harsh," Manuel says.

"Are you okay, Mr. Wright?" I ask, ignoring his comment.

"Oh, I am fine, darling, and how many times will I have to tell you to call me dad or uncle? You're my segunda hija."

"Sorry, dad," I shyly say.

My heart warms at what he said. Not even my own father was that gentle with me.

"So, nothing's hurting you?"

"No."

"Then why you're here, if you don't mind me asking?" I ask, sitting beside him on the couch.

He looks intently at me and sighs as if he's contemplating whether to tell me or not. I have never seen this look on his face before and I feel that it isn't something that I am going to like.

"Uncle?" I furrow my eyebrows in confusion.

Is it that hard to tell me?

"Mi hija, I am leaving prison."

My eyes widen as happiness wash over me. "Oh my god, you're being let out?"

He avoids looking at my eyes, which makes my smile drop.

"No, mi hija," he replies, now looking into my eyes. "I am escaping."

This time, my eyes widen in shock and fear. Manuel Santos, the boss of the Spanish mafia, is escaping prison and he's telling me.

He trusted me enough to tell me about his plan.

"Why...why are you telling me this?" I ask, my breathing getting heavier by the second.

"Because I need your help."

"I-I can't help you, uncle," I whisper. "How would I even do that."

"Look, I don't want to put you in a rough situation, but you are the only person who could help us."

"Us?" I exclaim.

"My two boys are here with me as well. Have been for a month. They came to rescue me."

"Uncle...I c-can't..."

"All you need to do is forget to lock your door."

"May I ask what you did to be here?" I ask, ignoring what he said, or rather not commenting on it.

He sighs heavily before saying, "I didn't do anything. I am here because I was set up, and because of my name."

"So, will you help us?" He asks when I didn't say anything.

I look into his fatherly eyes and couldn't help but nod. "I will help you, uncle, but only because you're like a father to me."

"And you call me uncle." He scoffs.

I smile sheepishly at him.

"Now may I ask why you decided to help me when you know that you might get in trouble?"

"When I think about it, I'd rather help a mafia boss than the police," I say, making him chuckle.

"Smart girl," he says with a smile. "Now, I won't pressure you for this, but I'd like to offer you a job when I get out."

"A-A job?"

"Yes. I'd like you to work for my mafia...as their doctor. Just think about it, you don't have to answer me now."

"Thanks, uncle."

"It's weird...the guards didn't come to check on you," I add in confusion.

"Oh, that's because my boys are giving them a hard time so I could take my time." He smiles, giving my a pat on the shoulder. "I will see you soon, mi hija."

"When are you...leaving?"

"Tomorrow. Tomorrow night."

It is the next day. I arrived early to prison.

I gave George his daily shot and sat doing nothing.

I start to get nervous thinking about what will happen tonight. A part of me hopes it works out for them and they escape. The other part says that I shouldn't help them and instead, should tell the police about their plan.

But I can't do that.

Manuel Santos is a father figure to me, even if I met him a few months ago. When he first came here, he had a heart problem. If I wasn't a surgeon, he would have been dead now. I had to request the prison to give me equipment to perform a surgery on him. They didn't agree at first, saying that he is to be transferred to the hospital, but Manuel didn't agree. It was either me, or no one.

He was the first patient I did a surgery on after quitting Life Hospital, and it will be the last.

I am still shook that I didn't shake while performing the surgery. I have trauma and I don't think it will go anytime soon.

If he hadn't insisted on me doing the surgery, I wouldn't have done it.

When the shift ended, I left the door open just like he requested. I am scared that the chief will find out that I purposely let the door open, but I would tell them that it was an honest mistake. After all, how would they escape their cells and where are the guards?

I reach my apartment and walk in.

Placing my stuff on the side table beside the door, I make my way to the kitchen, and prepare dinner.

I try to take my mind off Manuel's plan, but I couldn't. I am too afraid and I pray that he'll escape safely.

The fact that he told me his plan willingly and considered me as his daughter, makes me feel special. If he had killed an innocent person or committed other crimes, like crimes against women and children, I would have told the chief about his plan. But he was set up. But again, he's a mafia boss and I am sure he did a lot of horrible things.

But I couldn't say no. I couldn't not help him. He is the father I wish I have.

As selfish as it sounds.

The next day, I received a call from the chief of Central Prison. I immediately made my way to his office as soon as I reached.

He had five police officers with him, discussing god knows what.

"What happened?" I ask, acting stupid.

"Ana, three prisoners escaped prison through your room, which was unlocked for the first time! Care to explain that?" The chief yells.

"Are you insinuating that I helped them escape?" I gasp, making him avoid my eyes. "How could you! I forgot to lock the door and it isn't the first time. I think you should address your guards who are supposed to guard them!"

"Ana, these are dangerous people! Please tell me you had nothing to do with it, considering that your were close with Manuel Santos."

I try to calm myself down but my heart doesn't help.

"I had nothing to do with it, sir. My job here is to save lives and I gave an oath, did you forget?"

He nods hesitantly before saying, "I trust you, Ana. You can go back to your room."

"Thank you, sir."

With that, I leave his office and walk to mine. A part of me is still afraid that they'd find out what I did, but the other part is very happy that Manuel's escape was successful.

A guard walks into my office with George trailing behind him, handcuffed.

"Sit down," I say, rolling my eyes.

I give him his daily shot and send him back. George's body suffers from low vitamins and nutrients. He doesn't eat much. We used to give him serums, but he stopped taking them, saying that they take too much of his time. So instead, I designed these shots for him.

When I finished my shift, I drive back home.

My apartment is thirty minutes away from my workplace. It's a good and a bad thing. Good because when I go back home I forget everything about work and the neighborhood is entirely different. Bad because there's too much traffic in the morning.

I place the key into the keyhole and twist the handle, opening the door.

Weird...I left one light on.

I turn on the lights and turn around, only to be met with four figures, one of them extremely hot.

Chapter 03 - Change of Heart

I look at the four men in front of me, one of whom I recognize. I drop my bag accidentally from the shock as I stare at them.

My mind can't wrap around how they got in and I don't know what to say. I just stand and stare at them, waiting for at least one of them to speak up.

And thank god, one did.

"Mi hija, it's good to see you out of that place."

As if what he said broke me out of my frozen state, I say, "Uncle, what the fuck are you doing here? You shouldn't be here! What if they were following me? They asked me if I helped you today, and I told them no, but what if they didn't trust me?" I start rambling, scolding him like a little kid.

He smirks and looks at the man to his right, the hot man. "Te dije que Ella es diferente."

-I told you she is different.

"Veo que," the hot man replies, adding a smirk of his own.

-I see that.

"What are you saying, you know I can't understand Spanish," I say, narrowing my eyes at Manuel and the other man.

"My hija, I apologize for intruding on your home, but I couldn't help but come here because the police are everywhere."

"I-It's okay...but what makes you think that they won't come here?" I ask, walking further into my apartment, and reaching the couch, finally sitting down.

"Look at you, you look innocent, no one will even suspect you," Manuel replies as he sits down and tells his men to sit as well.

"But it is still not safe. You have to be careful," I insist.

"Well, mi hija, is it okay if we stayed for two days?" he asks.

"Of course! You can stay as many days as you want."

"What about your parents or friends?" the hot man asks.

When Manuel used to visit my office, we mostly talked about my family. He didn't open much about himself, but he did tell me that he has a wonderful wife and two kids. I mostly talked about myself because he used to ask a lot of questions. I told him everything but never told him about the hospital incident. But he knew that my family never supported me working at the prison.

"I don't have any, don't worry."

"Where are they?" one of the other two men said. He has brown chestnut hair with blonde highlights. I would never dye my heart like that, but it looks so good on him.

"Cash!" Manuel scolds.

"It's okay..." I say. "They...well, we aren't close and I haven't seen them in six months. "Anyways, I have two extra bedrooms, you can stay there," I add, changing the subject.

"Thank you so much, Ana. Also, think about my offer, will you?" Manuel says.

"You're welcome, and I will." I smile and leave to my room but not before telling them goodnight.

The next day, I woke up early.

I step out of the covers and make my way to the bathroom. I take a shower, washing my hair with my vanilla-scented shampoo and conditioner, and washing my body with my usual blueberry-scented body wash. When I finish, I wrap a pink towel around my body and walk out. But as soon as I do, I scream as I see a man in front of me.

Suddenly, all the events from yesterday come back to me. My eyes widen in shock as I wrap my arms around my body, running quickly to my room.

That's embarrassing.

I quickly put something on and walk out of my bedroom. I see the four men sitting in the living room and drinking coffee as if this house is theirs.

I glance at the hot man, who I still don't know his name, only to see him already looking at me. He's the one who saw me half naked a few minutes ago. Oh god.

"Ehem, good morning," I say.

"Good morning, mi Hija. Slept well?" Manuel says, placing his cup on the table and looking at me.

"Yes, thank you, how about you? Did you sleep comfortably in the rooms?" I ask everyone but only look at Manuel.

"Yes, thank you," Cash replies as the rest nod.

"So, may I know your names since you're staying in my house?" I ask politely.

"Of course! I am Cash," Cash starts, pointing at himself, "This is Alex; my older brother," he points at the other man who has not said anything since he came, "And this is Rafael," pointing at the hot man.

"Rafael is my son, mi hija," Manuel adds.

"Oh, really! I didn't know," I say with a grin.

He told me a lot about his family, yet he never told me his names.

"Well, I am Ana. I'm sure you all know that" I timidly say.

I get shy in front of hot men, who doesn't?

"Any news about the police?" I ask.

"No. They're still searching everywhere," Rafael replies.

"I better start getting ready for work. Don't want them to suspect anything," I say, standing up.

"Ana." Manuel stops me. "If anyone gives you trouble there, just tell me their name, sí?"

"Don't worry, uncle. No one can give me trouble, you know everyone loves me," I say with a grin, making him chuckle.

"Oh, I know, but still. Be careful."

"Will do." I nod and head to my room to get ready.

When I arrives at the prison, it was in chaos. Police officers ran around, trying to figure out what they have to do to catch them, chiefs panicking, scared of the bigger heads, and guards were placed everywhere, making sure the mistake doesn't occur again.

I walk into my office only to see chief Johnathon sitting in one of the chairs.

"Good morning," I say, looking at him in confusion as I put my bag on my desk.

"Good morning, Ana. Have a seat."

"Is there something going on?" I ask, sitting on my chair.

"I am afraid so. One of the guards told me that he brought Manuel to your room, but you didn't let him stay," he starts, making my heart beat faster. "He told me that he suspects you helping Manuel, and he told the chief of prisoners authority. He is coming to question you tomorrow."

"I have nothing to hide, Johnathon. I only did that because Manuel Santos doesn't like to speak in front of guards, and as a doctor, I have the right to hide my patients' records."

"No, Ana. You do not have that kind of right in here. You are not working at the hospital anymore, this is a prison!" His voice booms throughout the room. "I do trust that you had nothing to do with their escape, but not everyone thinks that way."

"Why would I jeopardize my job for a criminal? Are you insane!"

"You'll have to convince the chief tomorrow morning, and not me."

"Fine!"

When he left my office, I had the time to think of what am I going to do. The only thing that I feel I could do is ask for Manuel's help. But the thing is that right now, he's the one who needs my help, but we can't afford that anymore. I wouldn't be surprised if the police came and searched my house.

God, what did I do?

When I finished my shift, I drove back home.

I walk into my apartment and see Manuel sitting with his son, talking.

"Any news?" Manuel asks as soon as I stepped foot into the apartment.

I place my back on the dining table and sigh. "We...we need to leave as soon as possible."

"What happened?" Rafael asks, furrowing his brows.

I swallow hard as I sit beside Manuel. "The chief just spoke to me and told me that a guard suspected that I helped Manuel and the rest escape. This guard told the chief of prisoners' authority, and he is coming tomorrow to question me. If we don't leave, I am sure they'll come and search my house."

"Ana...why are you saying 'we'?" Manuel asks with a low voice as he narrows his eyes at me.

"I am coming with you...if that's okay."

"What do you mean, Ana?"

"I accept your offer, uncle. I want to work for you."

"But you do know that your life will never be the same, right?"

"I know."

"Why the sudden change of heart?" Rafael asks.

"They will find something and put the blame on me, I know that! Besides, I am not better than you!" I reply just in time as Cash and Alex walk into the living room.

"What do you mean?" Rafael asks.

I look at the four of them and then lower my gaze to the floor.

"I...I killed a man," I start, raising my head and looking at them again, "on purpose."

Chapter 04 - Igual Que Tú

"Ana? What happened?" My father asks as Ana trembles.

When she said that she had killed a person before, I thought that she meant accidentally since she's a doctor and sometimes things happen. But I didn't expect her to kill a person purposely, certainly not after my father talked about her since we have been here.

"I-I don't want to talk about it, but just know that I am just like you. But forget that because now, we need to get out of here because if they suspected anything, they will look into my past and I am afraid that they would find something this time."

"Fuck..." I mumble as I pace around the living room. There is no way we could reach our house without the police catching us. All the exits are surrounded by police at the moment, looking for my father. If we so leave this apartment, they would catch us. But at the same time, Ana might become a suspect, and her house will be searched. It is just all messed up.

"We need to leave, tonight," I announce as I stop pacing.

"But it's dangerous!" Alex exclaims, earning a glare from me.

"It's not if we play it right. No one even knows where our house and warehouse are. We only need a plan to drive past el control without being recognized," I reply.

"And how would we do that?" Ana asks, arching her eyebrow, and placing her hand on her hip.

"Well," I start as I walk around the four of them, "We change our appearances, get fake IDs, and get a cute minivan."

"We already have fake IDs," Cash points out.

"Great, then we will have to get one for Ana," I reply.

"How?" Ana asks.

"Leave that to me. We need one by tonight. In the meantime, we," I point at Ana and me, "need to go to the shop and get some things to change the way we look, like hair dyes and clothes."

"Hair dye? What the fuck dude! I won't dye my beautiful hair!" Cash exclaims.

"Shut-up. You won't even have to change your appearance because you will hide at the back of the minivan with Alex and dad," I snap at him.

"Would you please share your brilliant, detailed plan since we are getting so confused?" Ana asks sweetly.

"Ana and I would look like a married couple, who are going on a vacation to the outskirts of the city. I don't think they would search the van if they saw us as a lovely, so in love, extremely sweet couple," I reply sweetly, just like she did, giving her a fake smile.

"Married? You?" Cash snorts. "I can't imagine that," he adds and then laughs.

"Callar!" I say, glaring at him. Sometimes, I think of taking out my gun and shooting him between his eyes. That's how annoying he is.

-Shut up!

Cash puts his hands up in surrender, too afraid to say another word because he knows I'll fucking shoot him right here right now.

"Are you okay with that, my hija?" my father asks Ana, who is in deep thinking.

"I guess," she replies, unsure.

"It's settled then. Ana and I will leave right now to get the stuff," I say, clapping my hands together, then walking towards the door to leave. I opened it and waited for Ana to walk before me.

We walk beside each other as silence follows. None of us talk as we enter the elevator.

Ana presses the Ground floor and the door closes. As we wait, the awkward silence increases, but as soon as the elevator's door opens, we are surrounded by many voices, those who belong to her neighbors.

I subconsciously take her hand in mine and guide her through the crowd that happened to have gathered in front of the elevator as they discuss what appeared as an important topic.

I don't notice my grip on her hand when we left the apartment building, but she did as she took her hand out of my tight grip.

She doesn't say anything and walks faster in front of me until she stops in front of a weird-looking store close to her apartment.

She walks in as I trail behind her. A whiff of her smell invades my nostrils and my eyes involuntarily close.

Lilies.

I take in her beautiful smell and seem to be lost in it. I have never smelled something like this on anyone.

"We need to hurry," she says.

I nod and follow her blindly. She stops at the hair dyes section and we pick out a couple of cheap hair dye boxes of different colors.

This store had cheap stuff but it does the job.

After the hair section, we walk to the clothing section. They have so many different pieces that no one likes to wear, but we have to pick out something.

"What do you usually like to wear?" She asks as her hand goes through the different pieces on the rack.

I look disgustingly at the clothes and say, "Nothing like these."

She sends a glare my way and picks out a plain red t-shirt. "You will wear this," she says with a smug face and goes to pick out a pair of dark jeans, and says, "-and this."

I take them from her with an annoyed look as I see her look through the shoes. She picks out a black converse-looking-like shoe and throws them at me.

I send her a glare, one that she ignores as she walks to another section to get stuff of her own.

After thirty minutes, we finally walk out of the store. Our walk back to the apartment was fast, but before we could enter the building, Ana freezes as she looks ahead.

"What?" I ask.

She turns my way with widened eyes and says, "My chief, he's standing in front of the building."

"What the fuck is he doing here?" I growl, tightening my grip on the bags in my hands.

Before she could answer, her phone vibrates in her hand.

"He's calling." She holds her phone up for me to see. I grab her arm and walk somewhere he wouldn't see us.

"Yes, chief?" She says after answering the call. "No, I am out." "Yes...yes." "Okay, bye."

"What does he want?" I ask.

"He wanted to see me before tomorrow."

"Why?" I ask in confusion.

"He probably wants to check if I am okay." She shrugs.

"Let's head back," I say and walk towards the building. IAfter checking he is nowhere to be seen, we walk further and walk into the building.

Pressing the third floor, we wait till we reach Ana's apartment. When we do, the scene in front of us sends waves of shock to Ana and I.

Chapter 05 - Bienvenido a Casa

"You lied to me Ana," chief Zeke points out.

I make my way inside the apartment with Rafael following behind. The atmosphere was so awkward that I didn't know what to say.

"I am sorry," I say, dropping my head to the floor. I was so ashamed of what I did. "Please..."

"Please what, Ana?" His voice is firm and stern. "Let you go without taking you in? Letting them get away with murder as if nothing happened?" He questions.

I say nothing. I didn't even know what to say.

He looks around at all of us with a frown. We definitely looked like a family trying to get away with a criminal offense.

He shakes his head in disbelief and says, "You have got thirty minutes before I call the station."

Our eyes widen in shock and disbelief.

He's letting us escape?

"I will never forget this," Manuel says.

"I am only doing this for Ana," chief Zeke replies, earning a nod from Manuel.

We quickly pack everything and leave the house. We didn't even have time to dye our hair, so we had to go with hats and scarves, things that probably look suspicious, but we had no other choice.

The guy Rafael called while we were at the shop to get us a van and finally brought it to the apartment. So when we left, we saw the blue van waiting for us outside. The keys were left on the driver's door, on the inside.

"We have to leave. Dad, Cash, and Alex hide in the back, and let's hope they don't search the car," Rafael instructs. "Ana, you and I are a married couple, who are going for a road trip outside of town." He adds. I nod and we all leave, but not before I thank Zeke for his kindness. I wanted to ask him why was he helping us, but I didn't have time.

We hopped into the mini yellow van Rafael rented when we were at the store as he called the man on the phone and told him to deliver it as soon as possible.

After making sure everything was according to plan, Rafael starts the car and drives off.

"Where do you live?" I ask, looking forward at the road while I fidget with my fingers.

"Burnaby."

"Oh, it's very close. Are you sure there will be checkpoints?"

"I don't know, but since their escape, the police are everywhere."

"I hope not."

The first twenty minutes were going smoothly until I looked up and saw a checkpoint.

"Rafael, a checkpoint!" I quickly say in fear.

"I could see, Ana," he scoffs.

I roll my eyes at him and embrace the fear within me as he stops in front of the police officer.

Rafael rolls the window down and smiles at the officer. The officer just looks at him with no emotions as he asks for the IDs. Rafael takes him out and I give him mine. Rafael managed to get his form to get me an ID the same day.

The officer inspects them for approximately three minutes when he finally gives them back.

"You may go," he says in boredom.

Rafael didn't waste time as he sped off.

"For a second I thought he recognized us," I say breathlessly as I placed my hand on my chest, a sign of being scared.

"Mhmm..." He hums, not bothered to answer me.

Once we were in the clear, I started to breathe properly.

Burnaby is thirty minutes away from Vancouver, so the ride didn't take long.

Rafael drives through a tunnel that took us to a narrow road, away from the busy streets. This road leads us to a huge two-story villa with a massive garden. Two golden retrievers run toward Rafael as we walk through the giant golden gate.

Four bodyguards stood by the gate with walkie-talkies in their hands, an old style but effective.

"Welcome back, Mr. Santos." The guards bow their heads as they greet Manuel Santos.

"Hello, boys," Manuel greets with a nod.

We walk inside and I suddenly feel insecure. There are many guards scattered around as we walk inside the villa.

I was the only girl amongst them.

As we walk inside, I notice the simple, yet luxurious entryway that screamed traditionally.

It was so beautiful that I could look at it for hours.

My jaw hung low as I look around the interior of the house. If Manuel didn't usher me to go further into the house, I would have stood in my place and looked around the house.

"Rafael, are you sure the police won't look for us here?" I ask as I follow the three of them.

"They won't because they don't know that this house is ours," he replies.

I give him a confused look but he doesn't see it. Instead, Cash caught my reaction and decided to speak up. "This house is registered by our mother. Her files in the government system show that she doesn't have kids. No one knows that she's our mother. That's why they won't even consider looking here unless someone ratted us out." He looks at Manuel when he said the last sentence.

"Oh, okay," I say with a nod.

We enter an office, and Manuel sits by the chair behind the desk while the rest of us stand. His office has a lot of maroon furniture, which tells me that his favorite color is maroon.

Manuel opens one of the drawers and takes out a cigar. He places it in his mouth and lights it up.

The smell was unbearable that I had to pinch my nose with my thumb and index finger to not smell the awful smell.

I hate cigars.

"Okay, first, I would like to welcome you, Ana. Bienvenido a casa, mi hija," Manuel starts.

-Welcome home.

"And second, there are things that we need to discuss you joining our family."

"What are they?" I ask, all of a sudden feeling nervous.

"Don't worry, nothing much. The only thing that you mostly need to do as soon as possible is to swear Omertà," Manuel replies.

"Omertà?"

"The code of silence," Rafael points out this time.

"What should I do?" I asked, fidgeting with my fingers.

"You will need to swear your allegiance and loyalty to the family and swear that you won't talk about the mafia to the police or anyone, and swear that the family secrets don't go outside. This includes police investigation or CIA," Manuel explains.

I nod, understanding.

"When will that be?" I then ask.

"Tonight."

Chapter 06 - Omertà

An hour later

"Are you sure we can trust her?" I ask my father, who is sitting behind his desk, smoking his awful-smelling cigar.

He looks up at me and frowns. "Yes, don't you?"

"I don't know her, dad. She was practically working for the police," I reply, moving my hands around and sitting on the chair in front of his desk.

"She is to be trusted, don't worry. Besides, she is also wanted by the police by now."

It's true. By now, the police is informed of our departure and her involvement in it. The good thing is that they could never find us here. This house is registered under my mother, who's registered as a single woman, with no kids.

She is currently visiting my grandparents in Spain and is coming next week.

"Did she make the right decision? And why would she help you in the first place?"

I have so many questions. I don't trust easily, especially when it has something to do with my family.

"Can I worry about Ana? Don't worry, son...anyways, how's everything going on with you and Carmen?"

Carmen. A name I loathe. We have been engaged for five long, agonizing months. Before my father got prisoned, he asked me to marry his friend's daughter so our mafias get stronger. I said no at first because I hated the idea of marriage and kids, but after thinking about it, I agreed. I would do anything for my father even if I had to marry a woman I don't love. I am not mad at him because I know he wants to see me happy, but I didn't have to get engaged and married to be happy. That's what he doesn't understand.

"Not good," I simply reply.

"Why? What happened?"

What didn't happen?

"Dad, her and I, we don't work. She's too clingy, gets jealous a lot, and only cares about what brand she wears. I don't want to be married to a woman like her."

He sighs in frustration, making me feel guilty about confessing what's been bothering me.

"Stay with her for another month, if she didn't change and you couldn't stay with her, I'll speak with Lionel."

"Thanks, dad."

"I am sorry for forcing you to get married to her," he says.

"You didn't force me, dad. Don't worry about it."

I don't do good with emotions. I was never in a relationship before and even when I was younger, I was very cold, despite my mother's attempts to make me feel something.

I was and still am a cold person.

Why?

I don't know.

"By the way, inform Cody that Ana will be working with him at our infirmary. I would have liked for her to work at our hospital, but her identity would not be hidden, anyone could find her."

"Okay. I'll talk to him," I say and walk out of his office.

An hour ago, we left Ana in her new room that we provided for her. Tonight, she will take the omertà oath and will join our mafia. There will not be a ceremony or anything, just a few of our most trusted men will be present in my father's office as they witness Ana take the oath. There have to be a few witnesses every time someone joins our mafia.

I remember when Cash joined, Alex was already in before him. Cash was a little bit startled when he learned what his brother does for a living, but soon thought that it was better to join than to live with abusive parents.

"Cody." My voice echoes through the hallway as I near the infirmary. I walk in and find Cody behind his desk, reading a medical file. He looks too focused as his eyebrows are crossed and his eyes narrow.

"Cody," I call again, finally grabbing his attention.

"Yes? Sorry," he replies, putting the file down.

"I am here to inform you that a new doctor will be joining as your assistant."

"What? Why? I don't need one. Sabi is helpful," he quickly replies.

"I know she is, but she's not even a nurse. Ana Wright is a surgeon, she will be very helpful," I persuade him.

"Fine. When will I meet her?" he asks, standing up and walking towards me.

"Tomorrow. She will be taking the oath today and will start first thing in the morning."

"Okay." He nods, adding a sigh at the end.

After I left, I went to my room and was greeted by Carmen.

"Carmen? What are you doing here?" I ask with furrowed brows and narrowed eyes. She looks extremely ugly with her heavy makeup that hides every feature of her face.

"I've missed you." She pouts, circling her arms around my neck and pecking my lips.

Damn it.

I push her away gently. "Carmen, I am busy."

"What's going on with you? And who's that?" She points at someone behind me. "I have never seen her here before."

I look behind me and see Ana standing uncomfortably, looking everywhere but at us.

"Go home, Carmen," I order.

"I want to stay with my fiancé," she says on purpose.

She does everything on purpose.

"I said I am busy. I will talk to you later."

"Promise?" She pouts yet again, giving me puppy eyes.

"Fine, now leave."

After she walked away, I turn around and look at Ana. She looks annoyed.

"Is there something that you want?" I ask, not really in the mood for any more drama.

"I just needed a towel..."

"Did you check your bathroom?" I ask.

"Yeah, there aren't any."

I nod and motion for her to follow me. I honestly don't know where the towels are kept, so I decide on giving her one of the ones in my bathroom. One that I never used before.

"Here you go," I say, giving her a red towel.

"Thank you." She takes it from my hand and hugs the towel while still standing.

"Is there something else?"

"Yes. What will happen when I take the oath?" She nervously asks.

"You will continue working in your profession just like before."

"Really?" She grins.

"Yes. We have an infirmary. You will be working as Dr. Smith's assistant. Is that okay with you?"

"Yes! Thank you so much." She smiles brightly, making my lips lift a bit.

I just nod and leave.

Standing beside the door, I look at my father, who is sitting behind his desk, Cash and Alex, who are standing across from me, and Ana, who is standing in front of my father's desk.

"Do you swear to remain loyal to the mafia?"

"Yes."

"Do you swear to protect your family even if you had to die?"

"Yes."

"Do you swear to remain silent and protect this mafia's secrets?"

"Yes."

My father nods and smiles. "Welcome to De Santos mafia, mi hija," my father says proudly as if she's his biological daughter.

"Thanks?" She awkwardly replies, making my father and Cash die from laughter.

"Ana, with us, you will always be protected. This is your family. A family that you never had, always remember that."

"Thank you, uncle." She hugs my father.

Before anyone could say anything, the door is slammed open and Cody enters in a hurry. "You need to see this."

All of us follow him to the living area. Once we reach, we find a group of men gathered in front of the TV.

"Dad?" Ana mutters as she looks at the screen. Her father stood behind the podium, talking about four criminals, her amongst them.

"Ana is no longer my daughter. She is associated with criminals and helped them escape. I didn't raise my daughter like that. I will do everything in my power to bring justice and help catch these criminals."

I see her reaction only to find her fave blank. She doesn't show anything and just watches her father speak about her as if she isn't his daughter.

"I will keep my phone open for any inquires and calls as I work with the police on this case. I hope the public doesn't associate my brands and cut them because of my daughter. I am a fair man and my daughter will be put behind bars because she is guilty. Thank you!"

When he finished his speech, Ana didn't move.

"Are you alright, Ana?" My father asks.

She doesn't answer. When he asked again, she replied, "I need some air. I will be outside."

Chapter 07 - Cody

I was so mad at Rafael yesterday. How could he treat his fiancé like that? I wanted to slap him so hard but refrained from doing so. He was so rude to her.

I walk into the living room only to see Rafael's fiancé sitting with Cash and Alex. The guys look uncomfortable as she speaks to them while they don't answer her.

Why is everyone rude here?

I walk further until she sees me. My lips lift into a smile as I walk toward her, extending my hand for her to shake. "Hello, I am Ana."

She looks at my hand and then at my face, and scoffs. She shakes her head and stands up. She bumps into my shoulder on purpose as she mutters some colorful words that are not appropriate at all.

Wow. I am glad they treat her that way.

Suddenly, I am not mad at Rafael. She deserved how he treated her yesterday. What a bitch.

"Don't mind her. She gets jealous of her own shadow," Cash says.

"I wonder how Rafael puts up with her," I say, shaking my head, only to earn a groan from Alex.

"Oh, no," Alex says and stands up, and leaves.

"Finally!" Cash grins.

"Finally what?" I ask in confusion.

"Finally found someone to talk to about Carmen."

Oh, no, indeed.

"I don't want to be in the middle of anything," I quickly say, lifting my hands in surrender.

"Oh, don't be a party killer--anyways, Rafael actually doesn't put up with her. She has been obsessed with him for two years, and only last month did they get engaged. Her father is Manuel's friend and thought it would be best for them to get married."

"So, an arranged marriage?"

"Yes. He was against this whole thing, but he did it for his father. He hates the word Carmen, but don't tell him I told you that."

"That's sad."

"What is?"

"Marrying someone you don't love," I say with a frown.

"Oh, don't worry. Raphael doesn't actually have a heart that beats for another girl. He is cold and has a heart made of stone."

"That's even sadder."

"Tell me about it." he sighs, shaking his head.

"Anyways, I better go to the infirmary. It's my first day working there," I say standing up.

"Good luck!" Cash grins.

"Thanks."

Yesterday, after watching my father on the television, I had to leave for some air. No one came after me, especially when I locked myself in my room and acted asleep.

I was so heartbroken yesterday, but then again, I didn't really care. I knew he was toxic and never loved me. To him, I was an investment that would give him popularity. He only cared about himself.

I brush off the thoughts as I walk into the infirmary. Rafael and the doctor whose name I still don't know are sitting and conversing.

"Good morning," I greet as I walk inside.

"Good morning," the doctor replies. Rafael just nodded.

"Nice to meet you, my name is Ana," I say, extending my hand for him to shake.

"Cody. Nice to meet you too," he replies, shaking my hand.

His hair is sleeked back, has a defined nose, and little full lips. His small green eyes shined under the intense light of the infirmary. His height is average, a little shorter than mine.

"So, what will I be doing?" I ask as I take a seat in front of Rafael.

"Well, I haven't really thought about it, but you could start by helping me around with patients." He moves his hands around, pointing at no one in particular.

"Yes, sure. I prefer to help around than to be responsible for anyone on my own," I reply nervously.

"Why? I heard that you're a surgeon," Cody innocently asks as he furrows his eyebrows. Before I could say anything, Rafael clears his throat and stands up. "Cody, there might be some-one coming in today. Don't let him die."

My heart flutters from fear. I joined a mafia and I keep forget-ting what they do for a living. I don't know exactly what they do, but I don't think Manuel is cruel enough to kill people. But again, I don't know.

"Who?" Cody asks.

"Someone who works for Storm."

"Fine."

Working with Cody was fun. He was very gentle and taught me a lot of things as I taught him as well. He was very nice to me, unlike Rafael, who barely glances my way. Not that I care. I learned that Rafael is very moody. He could be very nice one minute, and the next minute rude. I don't know what goes into his mind.

I shower before going to bed. I don't want to sleep because I am not ready to have more of those nightmares. It's the same one every time - I see him in the emergency room, order the nurse to prepare the operation room, prepare myself to go in, and work on him to keep him alive. But the end of the dream turns dreadful. Without anyone understanding what I was exactly doing, I cut one of his inner organs, causing him inner bleeding. I didn't know what I did until the monitor beeped and announced the time of death. It dawned on me that I killed him with my own hands. I did it on purpose because I had to. He caused me so much pain.

The nightmares from what he did to me, turned into the nightmares of what I did to him.

I put my head on the pillow and close my eyes, praying quietly that I don't have any nightmares for once. But before I fall asleep, I hear a knock on the door.

I peel my eyes open and step out of the bed. I open the door and see Manuel standing. "Uncle?"

"Mi hija, can I come in?"

"Sure." I open the door further, allowing him to enter.

"Did something happen?" I ask as I follow him further inside.

"No. I wanted to talk to you about something."

"Okay..."

He sits on the sofa and ushers me to do the same. I oblige.

"I wanted to make sure that you're comfortable at the infirmary. After what you told us in Vancouver, I thought working at the infirmary could be the wrong decision, but I didn't want you to stop working."

I sigh and smile at him. "I am fine as long as I don't do something extreme to a patient. I just...I just can't do it anymore. I shake, and then I remember."

"You said you did it on purpose, why, if I may ask?"

I avoid his eyes and look at something in the room. "I am not really ready to talk about it. Maybe one day."

"I understand, mi hija. I will be there for you when you want to talk about it. If you ever feel uncomfortable, please tell me."

"Thank you, uncle."

"And by the way, don't mind Rafael's actions. He just doesn't trust you easily and doesn't know you as I do. Just be patient with him, please."

I shake my head a little and smile, "Don't worry about it. I understand."

"Thank you." He gives me the warmest smile and stands up to leave. "Good night."

"Good night."

Chapter 08 - Suposiciones

It happened last year. The weather was cold and snow covered the entire city, of Toronto. We were sitting in the living room of our house with my father and mother. Uncle Ricardo Storm had a smile on his face, which, at the time, I thought was genuine. Too bad it turned out as evil as his heart.

The police barged through the doors and arrested my father for something he didn't do. He was convicted of first-degree murder of a police officer.

Uncle Storm, a nickname we gave him for his bravery, was an undercover police officer, helping us on the inside. We never thought that one day, he would betray his blood brother, let alone with murder.

My father confessed that he committed the crime, only because he was blackmailed by Storm. Storm had a video of me killing five men two years ago. The bastard had been thinking about it for so long. He only wanted my father gone and not me, an old matter between him and my father, that my father thought he was done with.

That's why we moved to Burnaby. Storm doesn't know where we live and we never saw him since that night. He quit and went into hiding, knowing that I will stop at nothing to kill him even if he was surrounded by thousands of police officers. He doesn't know my mother's real name, which the house is registered under. Not that we didn't trust him, but she didn't.

My mother always hated Ricardo and we still don't know why.

Shrugging my thoughts off, I focus on the man in front of me. Word was out that Storm had started a small gang and this man is one of them. I don't know if he is stupid or what, but he just opened the door for me to find him and kill him. He might be planning on something and trying to trick me, but it will never happen again.

"Where's your base?" I ask, tapping the silver knife on the palm of my hand. When he doesn't answer, I repeat. "I said, where's your fucking base?"

He looks up at me and spits. "I'm not telling you shit!"

"Really?" I grin, confusing him. "Okay, then." I raise the knife and stab his hand, earning an ear-piercing scream. "The next stab is going to be in your dick," I add, making his eyes widen in fear, not daring to blink.

"Now, answer me." I sigh. "Where is your gang's base?" I ask calmly as if I didn't stab his hand a minute ago.

"R-Richmond."

"Where in Richmond?"

"I-I can't...please, he'll kill me."

"I'll kill you if you didn't tell me. Why would you protect a man who doesn't care about you?"

"He...he has my family...please." The man pleads, but it did nothing to my cold, stone heart.

"Well, such a waste of my time," I say, stabbing his heart. "Send the body to Richmond...anywhere near an alley, but make sure no kids could see or walk around there."

My men nod and pick the body and leave.

I kept waiting for guilt to hit but nothing happened. I don't feel guilty, mainly because I know he was lying. Well, I am 80% sure, which leaves a whole 20% that I don't think would get me to feel guilty.

I go to Cody's office. When I enter, I see Ana sitting with him, which makes me look at them in confusion, not that there's anything to be confused about. They work together. But I felt like it was weird seeing them laughing together, especially when Cody takes forever to like someone.

Before I could say anything, Cody speaks. "Where is Storm's man?"

"Umm...he's a hopeless case, forget about him," I reply as I pick up one of Cody's tiny statues he's obsessed with.

"Leave that! And what happened?" He exclaims, snatching the statue out of my hand.

I look at Ana who seems too focused on our conversation and reply, "I'll tell you later."

I don't want to scare her but again, she did say that she killed someone intentionally when we were at her house.

"Ana, I'd like to talk to you," I say, flicking my index and middle finger in the air, motioning for her to follow me.

She nods and follows me outside of Cody's office.

I walk with her following me and go to the library. We have a huge library in the villa that was made specifically for me. My mother said that I used to love books when I was younger and read so many books. I feel that she exaggerated because I stopped reading just after I turned 17.

"Is something wrong?" Ana's soft voice echoes through the library.

"No. I only want to talk to you about your work. How do you like it here?" I ask as I sit on one of the reading couches and point at the other for her to sit.

"It's still the second day, but I like it so far. Cody is a great mentor even though he's a few years older than me," she replies, placing a hair strand behind her ear.

She looks shy and I have no idea why, but I like it.

"Good. If anything or anyone bothers you, tell me," I say, not looking at her.

"Sure..." she replies, confusion covering her beautiful face. "Is there something else you wanted to say?" She adds.

"Yes, but I don't think you're ready for that, yet."

"What is it?"

"We'll talk later, Ana."

"Fine...whatever," she replies, rolling her eyes in annoyance. "If there's nothing else, I should go back to work."

"You can go."

After she left, I sat for an hour alone with my thoughts.

Why would Ana kill someone? Was that the reason she stopped being a surgeon? What did that person do to her and who was that person?

The only explanation for her killing someone for the first time would be either he hurt one of her family members, like killed someone close to her, or did something to her, and since she's alive, the only reason would be he sexually assaulted her.

Could that be the case?

Either way, I can't talk to her about it without her wanting to talk about it. I feel that it should come from her whether she wants to talk or not. I shouldn't push her to tell me anything.

I cut my thoughts off and walk out of the library. The more I sat with my thoughts, the more I overthink, and I don't want that.

I go to my room and change my clothes. My chest was bare and I wore navy pajama pants.

I let my body fall on the comfy mattress and I immediately feel comfortable. But that doesn't last as the door opens and Carmen walks in. I look at the seductive look she's giving me and fight the urge to roll my eyes.

"What are you doing here, Carmen?" I ask.

"We haven't been seeing each other lately. I have missed you." She pouts, walking towards the bed.

"I am tired now. Leave."

She doesn't listen and instead, she undresses. She stands naked to my lazy eyes, trying to get a reaction out of me, and she did.

I sigh in defeat, only because I am stressed and need a release.

During the night, I wake up. I look to my left and see Carmen sleeping soundly. I gently push her arm away from my chest and get up.

I wake up every day at 4 AM for no reason, and since I can't fall asleep again, I spend my time sitting in the backyard with my dog, Cheddars.

I didn't name him, rest assured. It was my sister who did, Alba. She has been outside of the country with my mother before my father escaped. They are coming in two days.

I skip down the stairs and walk out to the backyard. The chilly weather hits my skin, making me feel goosebumps.

My eyes land on someone sitting on the bench. A girl.

As I walk closer, I recognize her.

"What woke you up at this time?" I ask, sitting beside her.

"I have been awake for a while, and to answer your question, the guest room is close to yours," Ana replies, no hatred in her voice.

"Sorry," I reply, scratching the back of my neck.

"It's okay." She sighs. "What woke you up?" She asks.

"I don't know. I am used to waking up at this hour," I simply say.

She hums as she looks ahead.

"By the way, I haven't thanked you."

"For what?" She looks at me in confusion.

"For helping my father and the guys escape, and for letting us stay with you."

"It's nothing...Manuel is good to me. He's the father I wished I'd have."

I only nod, understanding her. My father is a great man. He's involved in everything related to Alba and me. He never missed a birthday, never left us when we needed him, and never once yelled at my mother or us. He is the man I have always wanted to be.

I look at Ana and notice a small leaf stuck in her hair. I lean in and raise my hand to get it out of her hair, but when she sees my movements, she flinches and quickly moves away, confirming my assumptions.

"I am sorry, I just wanted to remove the leaf," I say, pointing at her hair.

"Umm...s-sorry, I just..." she struggles to explain.

Without saying anything else, she turns around and leaves.

Fuck me.

Chapter 09 - La Madre

It's days like yesterday that make me think of how complicated I am. Perhaps it is because of what happened to me, or because I am just naturally complicated. The embarrassment that I feel at the moment is too much that I don't want to see Rafael ever again. He probably thinks that I am too complicated and hard to handle, that he might doesn't even want to be my friend. Not that we were friends before, the man hates me.

Removing the duvet that's wrapped around my body, I lazily make my way to the bathroom. The dream I dreamt comes crashing down at me as I sit on the toilet and do my business. My father and brother, Andrew, were questioning me, demanding to know why I helped criminals escape. My father had a scowl on his face, while my brother had a sad look. He was always the gentle type, though he left the moment he could to escape my parents.

My father then grabbed my hair, making me scream in pain, as he pushed my face on the table, demanding answers. That's when I woke up.

I am not concerned about the police funding me as much as I am concerned about my father finding me. Not that he ever laid his hands on me, but I know that he would do emotional and mental damage...much worse than what the police would do.

Not saying that physical damage is less of a pain than mental and emotional damage. They're all worse than the other.

I flush the toilet and clean myself with water before washing my hands and brushing my teeth. My hair looks messy and disheveled.

I sigh before leaving the bathroom and getting ready for the day.

I pull out my favorite outfit, a crop-topped white blouse, high-waisted light blue straight jeans, and my lucky white air force.

It's considered a teenager's look, but who cares. Anyone can wear whatever they want.

I grab my white coat and walk out of my bedroom. The smell of French toast hits my nostrils as I make my way downstairs. I almost moan in delight at the smell. My legs involuntarily make their way to the kitchen.

The back of a woman standing beside the table catches my eye. Her beautiful brown shoulder-length hair looks shiny under the sunlight, but what catches my attention are her eyes. Just like Rafael's.

Beautiful forest green.

I see Manuel with a bright smile, helping the woman with the food. I look in awe as I see his eyes sparkle as if he's seen the most beautiful thing in the world.

"Good morning," I say with a grin as I look at both of them.

"Good morning, mi hija! Come, let me introduce you to my wife!" he excitedly says.

"Mrs. Santos, it's very nice to finally meet you," I politely say, raising my hand for her to shake.

She looks intently at me with narrowed eyes, making me feel as if I said something room, but then a smile covers her red lips as she grabs my hand and pulls me into a hug.

"So, you're the famous daughter Manuelito has been talking about nonstop."

Manuelito. I fucking love her.

"And you're the famous Victoria Manuel had been raving about," I reply, a wide grin spreading on my lips as I look at her slightly blushed face.

"Well, ever since he escaped, he has been telling me about you through the phone. I had to come and see for myself."

"I am happy that you're finally here." I smile at her.

Manuel looks around as he holds Victoria's hand, and says, "Where is Alba?"

"She's changing in her room. She will come at breakfast," Victoria replies, giving her husband a chaste kiss.

"I hope you like French toast," Victoria says, bringing her attention back at me and leaving her husband wanting more of whatever little attention she was giving him.

"I do. It smells divine," I say excitedly.

Before she could say anything, the sounds of footsteps invade the kitchen, grabbing our attention to them.

Rafael, Cash, Alex, and Alba, walk together, joining us. Alba runs to her father and hugs him. She keeps stressing how much she had missed him and how he is going to continue teaching her self-defense.

Rafael hugs his mother and kisses her forehead, while Cash and Alex hug her. They look like a beautiful family and for some reason, I feel like I shouldn't be here. It feels illegal, but I ignore the feeling because frankly, I have nowhere to go.

"Now that everyone is here, let's eat!" Victoria says. She tells the two maids that I haven't seen to place everything on the table.

"Hello, I am Alba." Alba smiles.

"Hello, I am Ana," I reply, reciprocating the smile.

We walk towards the dining table and take out seats. Manuel sat on the head of the table, while Victoria and Rafael were beside him on each side. After Rafael sat Alba and then Cash. Alex sat beside Victoria on the other side, and I sat beside Alex.

The maids start bringing the breakfast and placing them on the table. My mouth watered at the sight of the French toasts and the multiple other plates. I itch to reach for the food, but I refrain from doing so.

When everyone starts eating, I reached for the food, hoping no one is focused on me. I hate when I eat with a lot of people. When I was younger, my father used to always be at work during lunch and dinner. My brother Andrew was living in dorms with his friends, so we didn't see him that much. It was only me, my sister, Sarah, and my mother.

Imagine living with two people who have the same ugly personality and who always pick on you and how you look. Anything my mother used to say, my sister, imitated it. That's why my sister and I have a rocky relationship. I don't blame her. Living with a mother like ours was hard. Sarah tried to live her own life, away from the house, but it only made her crueler. I don't know whether it was because of our mother, or from her own experiences. She wasn't bad before, but she became worse when I decided to quit my job at the hospital.

I was close with Andrew until he decided to move out, leaving me alone with them. And don't let me start on my father.

Seeing this big family together, even though Cash and Alex are not blood-related, brings a smile to my lips. I feel lucky to be here with them.

"Mi hija, why aren't you eating?" Manuel asks. Everyone stops eating and looks at me.

"I must have daydreamed, sorry." I start eating, wanting to get rid of all the attention Manuel brought on me.

I could feel someone's gaze on me and when I look up, it turns out to be Rafael's. I still don't know what to feel about Rafael. One time he's nice and the other he's cold. I still don't know how to talk to him and act around him.

"Has anyone tried contacting you?" Alex stops eating and looks at me.

"I don't know. I left my phone at my apartment," I reply.

"The police must have investigated your parents," Cash adds.

I shrug. "I don't care."

My answer must have shocked Victoria because when I looked at her, a shocked expression adorned her features.

She doesn't know, it's okay.

After breakfast, we all walk to the backyard. A golden retriever I have never seen here before runs towards Rafael and jumps on him. It is the first time that I see Rafael smiling.

The dog then skips toward me and starts sniffing.

"Hey," I gently say, kneeling to his level and petting his head.

"He's a sucker for girls," Alba comments.

"What's his name?" I ask, enjoying the feeling of his soft fur against my hand.

"Cheddars," she replies, sneaking a look at Rafael, who has a scowl on his face.

"Cheddars? Did Rafael name him?" I giggle, covering my mouth with my other hand.

Alba joins me, while Rafael's scowl only deepens. "No, I did, but Cheddars is Rafael's dog I got him on his birthday a few years ago. I made him get used to the name that Cheddars didn't listen to my brother when he called him Leo," she explains.

"Leo...such name guys would name their dogs," I reply.

"I know!" she exclaims, shaking her head.

The sound of footsteps cuts our conversation. I look to my right, only to freeze in my place upon seeing the person standing by the backyard's entrance.

Chapter 10 - Andrew

It takes me a moment to register what's happening. The fact that I thought my brother had graduated and is staying with his friends, makes me feel like I'm a fool. He hadn't been visiting, maybe once or twice a year, and barely calling. Indeed, he took his time to graduate, which is totally fine, but he completely ignored our existence, my existence.

I look up at his shocked face and anger fills my body. All this time, he has been what? Working for the mafia?

"Ana..." His voice is shaking as he looks at me with guilt.

I look around to see if anyone knew, but from their shocked faces, I don't think they did.

"You know her?" Rafael asks, furrowing his brows.

Andrew swallows and nods. "She's my sister. The one I told you about."

I hear someone cursing, but I don't know who. The only thing I could think about is how angry I am.

I look at Andrew with the fire burning in my eyes. I still can't comprehend what's happening. How is he here? The fucker left us, let me, and joined a mafia. Why? What happened to him? He left us and we never knew anything about him. The only times he comes back home were on Christmas and New Year. Not even our birthdays.

"Ana...please say something," Andrew pleads, keeping a good space between us.

I want to hit him, yell at him, and make him feel like shit, but the only thing that I do is answer him coldly because I don't want to show him how much he hurt me.

I look around the room and my eyes land on Rafael's gun. Oh, how much I want to shoot Andrew's leg to take my revenge. The funny part is that Rafael saw me looking at his gun and he tightens his hold on it, thinking that I'd actually use it.

I look back at Andrew, who still has a pleading look on his face, and say, "Well, what do you want me to say? Nice to see you, bro?"

I glare at him and march inside the house, leaving him outside. The tears which I suppressed start coming down. I run to my room and start crying my eyes out.

I feel betrayed, humiliated, and hurt.

I tried. I tried leaving the house, but my father was a control freak. He let my brother go because he was a boy. Boys could do anything they want, according to him. Besides, he loved Andrew more. Andrew is two years older than me. I used to cling to him whenever I was scared of my parents. He knew that. He knew how much they expected from me and when I couldn't deliver what would happen. Yet, he left. He left to live the life he wanted, away from my parents. I shouldn't blame him, but I can't help but feel betrayed and hurt.

I was alone in that house.

I keep sobbing that I don't hear the door opening. I feel a hand around my shoulder, making me flinch slightly.

"Hey, it's me," Victoria says, making me relax.

I look at her and bury my face in her neck as I continue crying. She pats my back gently, not telling me to stop. She's letting me take it all out, which I am very grateful for.

When my cries die down, she takes my face in her hands and wipes my tears with her thumb. "Are you okay?" Her gentle voice soothes me.

"Yes," my voice cracks.

"Now, tell me, darling. What happened out there?"

I sniff and push my body backward, so I could look at her properly.

"Andrew is my brother. He...left a few years ago to live on his own. We never really see him unless on Christmas or New Year. We were very close and he left."

"Why did he leave?" She frowned, gently playing with my hair.

"My parents...they are too much. I know I am acting like a selfish person, but I can't help but feel betrayed. He left me with them, knowing how they treat me. The only time I finally got out of that house was when I quit the hospital. I finally got to live on my own for six months until now."

"Come here, honey." She hugs me tightly and plays with my hair gently. "I am sure he has an explanation. Hear him, okay?"

"I shouldn't blame him nor be mad at him. It's his life and he could do whatever he wants. I just thought that he would act differently because I'm his sister."

"I know, sweetie. I know." She breaks the hug but still holds me close as she looks into my eyes. "I have known Andrew for a long time. He studied with Rafael at the university, and as far as I know, he has reasons for everything. He used to always talk about his sisters. We never really asked anything personal about his life because he used to get mad, but he never stopped talking about his one sister that he missed the most."

For some reason, hearing Victoria telling me about how Andrew talked about us made me feel so much better. I feel like I wasn't the only one who thought about him. He did too. He never forgot me.

"Thank you, Victoria." I smile weakly, hugging her again.

It's so weird that I felt Victoria like a mother to me when I just met her half an hour ago. I didn't even feel this way with my mother. Manuel was so right about her when he told me how kind his wife is. She's an angel.

She smiles back and wipes my tears again. "I know you don't feel like going back down, so stay here and I'll speak with Andrew."

"Okay, thank you."

She nods and smiles, and walks out of the room.

I push my body back on the bed until my back hits the comfy mattress. I close my eyes and sigh deeply. My eyes hurt from how hard I cried. They're burning.

I walk to the bathroom and wash my face, massaging my eyes gently. I always did that whenever I cried as if the pain would miraculously go away. It's amazing how different every person deals with pain.

I decide to take a shower. Showers are the only thing that could make you feel better besides food. Not every person has an appetite after they cry or feel sad.

After showering, I wear my pajamas and head to bed. It's still very early, but I can't open my eyes. They still hurt.

I cradle the duvet and let sleep consumes me.

When Andrew and I met in university, we never went deep into our families, especially me because I couldn't tell him anything about my family, so he never told me about mine and I never asked. It was only when we became best friends that he told me about his, and even then, he never went too deep. I knew his parents and their names, but he never told me his sister's. I didn't even tell him about Alba.

When he joined the mafia, he met my parents and Alba, and even then, I never asked him about his family because I know it was a hard subject for him.

"How...why is she here?" Andrew asks with a frown on his face.

We are sitting in the backyard. My mother, father, Cash, Alex, Alba, and Andrew.

"It's a long story," Cash says.

"What happened?" Andrew asks.

"She's the doctor that helped us escape," I reply.

"I know that, but why is she here? I thought she helped you and that's it," Andrew explains.

"Well, she insisted to come," Alex speaks up.

"She? She insisted?" Andrew's eyebrows lift in surprise.

I nod. "You need to talk to her."

"She won't listen."

"I talked to her and convinced her to listen," my mother points out.

Andrew just nods, not saying anything. I could feel his anxiety through the air as his leg moves up and down.

"I better go. I'll come back later to talk to her. Don't let her go."

"Don't worry, she's staying here," my father replies.

Andrew nods and leaves.

I decide to go check up on Ana even though I give no shit about her. Well, yeah...

I knock on her bedroom door and wait till she opens it. A minute goes by and she doesn't open the door. I decide to call for her name. Again, she doesn't answer.

I put my hand on the handle and open the door slowly. I look inside only to see her on the bed, sleeping. I walk inside like a thief until I stand beside her bed. I see the duvet's not covering her stomach, so I pick it up and cover her.

She suddenly moves and mumbles something. I quickly walk out, but not before hearing a scream from behind me.

Chapter 11 - Mrs. Victoria Santos

"You scared me! What are you doing here?" Ana scolds me, getting out of bed and standing in front of me. "I thought you were an intruder!"

"Calm down. I just came to see if the windows are closed," I say with a scowl on my face.

"Why would they even be opened?" She asks, putting her hands on her hips.

"It doesn't matter. You can go back to sleep." I start making my way out, but a hand grabs my arm, stopping me.

"Rafael..."

"What?" I harshly reply, making her flinch a little bit.

I immediately feel bad because it wasn't what I intended to do, it just came out like that.

She glares and lets go of my arm. "Nothing! Get out."

I roll my eyes and leave, hearing the door slammed behind me.

Fuck, she's mad.

I go to my office, two doors away from Ana's room, the one beside my room. Only my office is located close to my room because of my lazy ass, but the rest are on the third floor.

I push the door open and walk in. My mother is already sitting on my chair, browsing through my laptop.

"Mamá, qué estás haciendo aquí?" I ask, walking further into the room. She looks mad as a frown adorned her beautiful face.

-Mom, what are you doing here?

She slams the laptop shut and glares at me. "I was passing by Ana's room and heard you two."

"Okay?"

"Okay? I raised you better than that, Rafaelo."

I hold back rolling my eyes because I don't want to be murdered by her. Trust me, she'll do it. "I didn't do anything, mama."

"You were rude!" she yells. "Didn't I teach you to be a gentleman?" she asks a rhetorical question, but I answer anyway.

"No..." I shake my head as a no, making her angrier. "I am joking!" I quickly say when I see her sad face.

I was joking, really.

"You will treat her better, Rafaelo, or I swear I'll tear you apart! Understood?" Her voice booms across the room, making goosebumps crawl on my skin.

"Yes, mamá." I nod.

"Good." With that, she walks out and slams the door shut, not caring who wakes up from the noise.

Fuck, she's really mad.

From a very young age, my mother started teaching me how to treat girls. I was doing great until Alba grew up and I had to punch every guy who looked at her the wrong way. That's when I threw everything my mother taught me away. I couldn't even treat Alba like a lady, mostly because I wanted a brother. We used to wrestle, train with one another, and curse at each other. I also used to annoy her a lot, making her wish she had another brother. I still do.

Alba is my favorite person after my mother. She's my best friend and partner in crime. she could be annoying sometimes, but there isn't a day that goes by that I don't talk to her.

And she's the only person I go to when I need to get something out of my chest.

I knock gently on her bedroom door and wait for her to open. After waiting for a few seconds, she finally opens the door. A sleeping mask is placed on her head as she looks lazily at me. "Rafa? What are you doing here?"

I sigh before saying, "Necesito hablar."

- I need to talk.

She opens the door wider and ushers me in. She sits on the bed and crosses her legs, giving me a sign that I could start talking.

"Well, mom is mad at me." I huff, burying my face in my hands.

"I kinda heard yelling, why?"

"She was passing by Ana's room and heard me speaking with her rudely. I didn't really do anything, just my tone was a little harsh."

Alba closes her eyes for a few seconds and then reopens them. "Rafa, you know how mamá acts when it comes to behavior. Why are you being rude to Ana? Did she do something?"

"No, she didn't. That's the problem."

"What do you mean?" Alba furrows her eyebrows and tilts her head.

"I...I kind of...well, I feel something."

"I don't get you, Rafael. What do you mean?"

"Fuck, do I have to say it? I have a crush on her."

"So, let me get this straight," she starts with a grin, "You have a crush on Ana, yet you are being rude to her, and that's why?"

"Alba, did you forget that I am engaged to Carmen?"

"Oh...yeah. I actually forgot." She chuckles, making me roll my eyes. "I have always hated Carmen, Hermano."

"Who doesn't," I mumble.

She sighs deeply before yawning. "Don't you want to break it off?" She asks.

"I want to, Alba. I told dad and he said that in a month if I still want to break it off, I could. But I know how much this marriage means to him and the mafia. I don't want to let him down."

"But Rafael, this is your life. You deserve to be happy. I am sure dad won't stand in your way, despite it being his idea to marry Carmen."

"I don't know what to do, Alba. I have never even been in a relationship other than with Carmen. I don't know what it feels like to love someone."

"Oh, trust me, it's the best feeling in the world," she replies with a smile, making me frown.

"Alba."

"Yes?"

"Who is he?"

"Who is who? What do you mean?" She quickly sits straight, avoiding looking into my eyes.

"Alba," I warn.

She yawns again and quickly says, "I am very tired and sleepy. Good night!"

She slips under the covers and waves at me like the idiot she is. I know what she's doing, I am not stupid.

"Fine. We will talk later, Alba. I won't forget."

I walk out of her room and go to mine.

Who the fuck could it be?

I try not to think about it as I try to sleep.

My phone suddenly pings, indicating that I received a message. I huff before grabbing the phone from my nightstand and unlocking it. I go to my messages only to see that Carmen left me one.

-Carmen: Quieres salir mañana?-Want to go out tomorrow?

I weight the pros and cons and decide to go out with her. It's the only option for me not to think about anyone else.

-Me: Okay.

-Carmen: Really?! Okay, my love. See you tomorrow.

-Me: See you.

The next day, I look for my mother to apologize to her. I hate when we fight or argue.

When I spot her standing behind the stove with Ana, I quickly make my way to her.

"Mamá."

She looks at me but doesn't say anything.

"Mamá, can we talk? Please."

She tells Ana to continue stirring whatever's in the pot and follows me outside.

"Si, Rafael?" -Yes.

"Lo siento."-I am sorry.

"About what?"

"Yesterday," I reply.

"I am not the one you should apologize to," she replies.

"Okay." I nod, walking back into the kitchen. Ana must have sensed my presence because she looks behind and her eyes landed on mine.

"Ana..."

"Yes?"

I walk further until I stand beside her. I take the spatula from her hand and stir the pot. "I am sorry about yesterday. I didn't mean to scare you, nor speak harshly with you. I was just mad and I shouldn't have taken it on you." It's a half lie.

She seems taken aback by my apology but quickly recovers. "Thanks...I guess. Anyways, it wasn't that big of a deal. I forgot about it."

Tell that to my mother.

I just nod and give her a small smile.

"So, you're working today?" I ask.

"Cody gave me a break today and said that there isn't too much work. He doesn't need me."

"Mhmm." I hum. "I think this is done," I say, turning off the gas.

"Thanks." She nods.

"Well, I'll see you later," I say and walk out of the kitchen. My mother is still standing outside as if she's waiting for me to give her a report on what happened.

"What wasn't so bad, was it?" She says, crossing her arms together.

I am thirty years old and I still get scolded, the fuck?

"Mom, did you see dad?" I ask, ignoring her earlier statement, earning a glare.

"Yes. The last time I saw him was in the backyard. He was watering the plants."

"Okay, thanks," I reply, turning around to leave, but stop, remembering to tell her something else. "By the way, Edwardo is visiting today."

"Okay, honey."

At dinner, my family's friend Edward, who works for the police station in Vancouver, came to visit. He's our undercover spy at the station, giving us reports every month on things related to the mafia. But since my father's, Cash's, and Alex's escape, he'll be visiting every week to give us updates on what the police find.

"Welcome, son," my father greets Edwardo.

"Thanks, papá. How are you?"

"I am alive." He chuckles.

"Come on inside!" My mother's cheerful voice brings a smile to everyone's lips.

We all sit around the dining table, minus Cody and Ana. After a few minutes, they came down together.

"Oh, Edwardo, this is the newest member of the family, Ana Wright," my father introduces Ana to Edwardo.

"Yes, head all about her at the station." Edwardo smiles, shaking Ana's hand.

"Nice to meet you, Edwardo," Ana replies.

Ana sits beside Cody across from me. She looks beautiful with her wavy chestnut hair and rose-colored cheeks. Her smile looks genuine, making her eyes pop. Overall, she looks gorgeous.

A tap on my thigh brings me back from my daydream. I look to my right greeting Alba's warning eyes as if she's telling me to stop staring because it's obvious.

"So, Edwardo, what's new?" My father asks.

"Well, they have searched Ana's old car and found someone's fingerprints, but not any of you. It traces Ana's father, Christopher. Ana, did you leave something in the car that your father wanted?"

Ana's face turns pale. She gulps and swallows hard.

"Ana?" My father calls.

"I...there's my book."

"Book? What book?" I ask this time.

"A book that's very important and cannot reach anyone's hand. We need to get it back." She panics.

"What's in the book, Ana?" My father asks.

"It's...my diary. If the police get it from my father, I'll officially become a murderer."

Chapter 12. The Plan

When I was ten, I told my parents that I wanted to become a doctor. They discouraged me, saying that it would take years to graduate to become one and that I should take an easier major because I am a girl. They wanted me to get married by the age of 25 because after that it would look bad for me and them.

When I grew up and it was time to go to university, I forced them to agree that I study medicine. They reluctantly did, thinking it would look good because my father was a surgeon as well.

When I finished early and started my residency, they kept telling me to get married to the point that my father brought his friend's son to meet me. I absolutely hated that arrogant jerk, Peter. He was annoying, self-centered, and haughty.

It wasn't until I finished my residency that my parents stopped forcing me to meet anyone else.

Working as a surgeon had been my dream, and still is. But I never thought that one day, I'd be killing instead of saving lives.

Killing on purpose.

"You need to elaborate more, mi hija," Manuel gently says, placing the fork and knife on the table and giving me his undivided attention. Everyone's attention is on me as they wait for me to explain.

"I told you...before in Vancouver," I say, not wanting to go deep into the matter, especially not in front of everyone.

"But we need to know what exactly happened so we could help you," Alex speaks this time.

"I killed someone," I blurt, shocking most of the people who didn't know, especially Victoria.

Victoria looks at me in disbelief as if she never thought that I am that kind of person. Alba doesn't look into my eyes, while the rest look normal.

"No one knows, not even the hospital."

"Why would you write a confession in a book?" Rafael asks.

"I didn't exactly write that I killed that man. I just wrote that it's my fault he's dead, which is basically the same thing. I wrote it in my book because I felt guilty and I couldn't tell anyone."

"Why? Why did you kill the man?" Victoria asks.

That's my secret and I never want to tell anyone. Besides, what if they didn't understand? What if they said that it wasn't enough to kill him? I don't even know these people, not even Manuel that much.

"I don't want to talk about it," I say, fidgeting my fingers in a nervous matter. I avoid looking at anyone, only hearing silence.

When I look up, my gaze landed on Manuel, who understood that I couldn't talk about it and nodded. "It's okay, we'll talk later. For now, we need to do something about that diary."

"Andrew." Rafael is the first to provide a solution that none of us understood.

"Andrew?" My voice comes out confused and bewildered.

"He's the only one who could go to your parent's house without anyone suspecting anything," he elaborates.

"But he hasn't been there since forever. It would definitely look suspicious to my father. He knows how close I was with Andrew, he'll know I talked to him and asked for help."

"No, he won't because the last thing Andrew told your father was that he was going to live in Argentina and get a new number. He even sent it to him."

"Argentina? Why would he lie about that?" I ask, totally disregarding the important topic.

Rafael glares at me, making me raise my hand in mock defense.

"Anyways, Andrew could go in, get the book, and comes out without anyone noticing anything," he continues.

"I am sorry I am dragging you all into this. What if the police find out, they link you with me?"

"They can't, there's no evidence," Cash points out.

I huff, burying my face in my hands. The last thing I want to drag this already fucked family into my mess. I know Manuel just escaped and the police are after him anyways, but still, I don't want to impose and I already feel out of place here.

"Don't worry, darling, it will be sorted out," Victoria says gently, making me feel a little better.

"Rafael, call Andrew and tell him about the plan. Cash and Alex, stay at the warehouse until further notice," Manuel fires orders. "...and Alba, I don't want to get you into trouble, but we need you right now."

"What is it, father? Tell me," Alba replies confidently.

"Drive to Vancouver with a fake ID and a new look. I need you to go with Andrew and act as his partner. It would look more convincing for his parents if Andrew came back with his girlfriend, wanting to introduce her to his parents."

I notice Alba's face flush and her cheeks turn red from embarrassment. I could tell she felt uncomfortable already.

My gaze shifts to the other side and I see Cash's clenching his jaw, almost breaking it. Rafael's face held a scowl, obviously not liking that his sister is going to act as a guy's girlfriend.

"Does she really have to do this?" Rafael tries his luck.

"Yes, Rafael. Don't question me."

Rafael nods and gets up to leave. Cash and Alex follow him behind.

"I am sorry you have to do this," I tell Alba.

"It's okay, darling. Besides, Andrew is hot."

"Alba!" Victoria and Manuel scold, making her giggle before getting up to leave.

"Kidding!"

The parents shake their heads in amusement while I smile at her antics. I have known her for what, two hours? And I already like her.

"What should I do?" I ask, getting their attention back at me.

"You do nothing, mi hija. Let us handle this one. Besides, there isn't anything you could do besides wait."

"You're right." I sigh.

At midnight, I get myself ready to sleep. I haven't heard anything from anyone yet, but I am sure tomorrow I will.

I wear my pajamas and get under the covers. It's a cold night and the duvet is not helping keep me warm.

I get up to get a jacket to wear when I hear footsteps outside my door. I furrow my eyebrows in confusion and walk to the door and pull it open.

"Rafael?"

"Hey, sorry, did I wake you up?"

"You didn't even knock." I chuckle.

"Well, I talked to Andrew and he's in. He will drive to Vancouver tomorrow with Alba and will visit your parents."

"I hope they find the book at the house."

"I hope so. Do you know where he might have hidden it if not at the house?" He asks, the little light coming from my room illuminating his face.

He is beautiful.

"It might be at his office at the hospital, but I doubt he'd leave something so important for anyone's reach. The nurses sometimes go into his room, so it's risky."

"Mhmm...if we didn't find it, what should we do?"

"I don't know Rafael...I guess I'll become a criminal." I chuckle sadly.

"Hey, all of us here are criminals, it wouldn't be so bad," he replies with a smirk.

I laugh, wholeheartedly. "You're crazy."

"I know." He grins as he looks at me with hooded eyes.

His forest green eyes look beautiful under the dim light and I can't help myself but stare at them. They are beautiful, and the way he's looking at me is making me feel weird things. Things I shouldn't feel.

"Umm...well..."

"Rafe!" A high-pitched voice echoes through the hall, not caring who's sleeping.

"Carmen?" Rafael looks at her in disbelief. "What are you doing here?"

"I have missed you." She pouts, grabbing his face and kissing him on the lips. "Didn't you miss me?" She asks, her eyes then land on me.

"You again?" She says.

"Carmen," Rafael warns. "Go home," he adds.

"But it's midnight! You want me to go back alone?" She protests.

"You came here by yourself alright."

Not wanting to stand there like a total freak, I mumble a good night and walk back into my room. I grab a jacket from my bag and put it on, already feeling much warmer. I could still hear their voices, arguing behind the door, but I try to ignore them and sleep.

When I hear footsteps going left and into Rafael's room, I become certain that she's staying the night.

I just hope I don't see her at breakfast tomorrow.

Chapter 13. Misión Fallida

One of the things I hate about Carmen is how much she nags. For example, I let her stay the night yesterday because I knew that if I didn't, she would keep on nagging until I agreed, so I saved my time and agreed immediately.

Sometimes I feel like I'm a mother.

I wake up the next morning feeling drained. I only feel this way whenever Carmen decided to sleep over. I just can't get used to sleeping beside her, especially when I feel awkward hugging her to being intimate with her. It just doesn't feel right.

I head to the bathroom before she wakes up and takes a shower. When I finish, I wear my navy blue suit to get ready for work.

Fortunately for me, no one knows what Rafael Santos looks like. I always take my fake ID whenever I go and no one knows the real me. It is one of the clever things my mother did when she married my father. She knew the life he was in and didn't want us to be involved in it. So, she married him secretly, registered us with fake names in the government, and made sure no one knew about that.

I have an Albanian passport, however; with my real name from the years I lived there.

When I left the bathroom, Carmen was wide awake.

"Good morning, baby," Carmen says, yawning. "This is the best sleep I have had, what about you?"

"Yeah...me too," I reply, not looking at her.

I style my hair quickly before she has the chance to climb out of bed and make her way toward me.

I open the door and leave her inside, whining.

I go to my father's office and enter without knocking. I was done with that shit.

"Rafa? What's wrong? Did something happen?" My father asks. Ana is sitting on the chair across from his desk.

"We need to talk," I firmly say. The look on my face looks alarming.

He narrows his eyes at me and nods. "We'll talk later, Rafael. We have important business now. Alba and Andrew arrived in Vancouver. Andrew called his parents this morning and told them that he was coming with his girlfriend. In an hour, he's going in."

I wanted to yell at him, saying that I don't fucking care about the mission, but I don't. I know he'll be sad and I don't want Ana to think that I don't care about her situation because I do.

"Fine." I bit back.

Ana is avoiding looking at me. She looks nervous and a little angry.

After waiting for almost an hour, talking about random stuff, Andrew's earpiece is finally activated, followed by Alba's.

"Can you hear me?" Andrew's voice blasts through my father's laptop.

"Yes, we do. Where are you now?" My father asks.

"We are still in the car. We just arrived," Alba says.

"Okay, be careful. Make sure to look convincible," my father warns.

We hear the sound of the car's door shut, followed by a doorbell.

"I am scared," Ana suddenly says.

"Don't be. Andrew and Alba are great at their jobs. They will get the job done," my father assures her.

"My baby!" We hear a woman's voice. I see Ana tense in her seat when she hears it.

"Hello, mom," Andrew replies.

"Oh, gorgeous girl! Hello,"

"Hello, Mrs. Wright," Alba replies.

"Oh, please, call me Michelle."

Ana rolls her eyes when she hears her mother, making me frown.

What happened that made her hate them so much? I think to myself.

After about thirty minutes, Andrew tells us that he's looking for the book, while Alba distracts his parents, and one thing you should know about Alba is that she a master when it comes to distraction. We always take her with us on missions because she's of great value to the team. My father doesn't like the idea of her coming with us, not because he thinks that she is weak or anything, but because she's his princess and he would die if anything was to happen to her.

What about me? Well, who am I when it comes to Alba? Nothing.

Nah, just kidding.

"I am in his office now." Andrew's voice blared through the laptop.

I see Ana fidget in her chair, waiting impatiently for the book to be found. I could tell she is anxious and nervous even though she is already guilty of helping criminals escape. But being guilty of murder in front of the public for something that she had to do, is worse.

"Ahh, found it," Andrew finally says, making Ana sigh in relief. "Who would put an important book on his desk for everyone to see?"

"Because everyone at home knew that no one was allowed inside. Are you sure no one saw you?" Ana replies.

"Yes, don't worry."

"Open the book and make sure it's the one. There's a flower painted on the first page."

We hear shuffling before Andrew replies, "It's the one, sis."

I could tell Ana fought hard not to reply with a sarcastic comment when he called her sis.

"We are leaving in ten minutes," Alba whispers.

"Be careful, mi amour," my father says.

Ana suddenly frowns, and I immediately know what she's thinking because I am thinking it too.

"This was too easy," Ana points out.

"What is?" my father asks.

"This...this mission. Why would my father leave the book on the table and the door unlocked? If I had something very important, I wouldn't want to take any chances," she explains.

"She's right, dad. I think her father knows that Andrew came for the book."

"Andrew, Alba, get out of there as soon as you can," my father orders.

"We are out," Andrew replies.

"I am so sure that my father photocopied the book," Ana says, burying her face in her hands.

"I am sorry, mi hija. We pulled you into this mess."

She looks up, and her eyes land directly on him. She gives him a small smile and says, "It's not your fault, uncle. It was my choice and I don't regret it."

A question rises in my head. Why would Ana help my father escape, destroying her career? What is she after?

My father nods in gratitude.

At midnight, Andrew and Alba arrived. He had the book in his hands when he came inside the house. He gave it to Ana, which she took without hesitation. It was only when she opened the book that her face paled.

"What's wrong?" I ask, crossing my brows.

"I told you. This was too easy," she says, whirling the book our way so we could see.

'I HAVE ANOTHER COPY THAT'S ON ITS WAY TO THE POLICE' is written in capital letters on one of the pages.

"Call Edwardo and inform him to take care of it!" I tell Cash, who takes out his phone quickly and dials Edwardo's number. "Alex, send some men you know from Vancouver to every police station. Make sure they look for anyone delivering a package."

"Don't worry, honey, we will take it before the police do," my mother tries to comfort Ana.

After a few minutes of silently crying, Ana storms out of the living room and walks to the backyard. I see Cheddars follow her like the softy he is.

Without anyone noticing, I slowly back away and walk to the backyard to make sure she's okay.

If I was in her place, I would be scared too. She maybe never did anything illegal in her life and then suddenly kill someone for something he did to her. I am certain now.

"Ana?" My voice is soft and gentle.

Her back faces me as she cries, while Cheddars whimpers beside her. When did those two develop a deep relationship?

"Please, I need to be alone."

I ignore her and sit beside her on the bench. I sigh as the wind gives me a whiff of the nature surrounding us. I look at her face and wipe the tears with my thumb. "I promise you, nothing will happen to you."

"How can you promise such a thing?" Her voice cracks.

"I can make people disappear."

She sniffs and asks, "Why are you even helping me?"

A deep frown settled on her face as she waits for my answer. I massage my temples, not wanting to give her the answers she's looking for, but she deserves it. "You helped my father, Ana. I will forever owe you."

"No, you don't. I did it because I wanted to."

"Why did you?" I ask gently, not wanting to sound rude.

She sniffs a couple of times and wraps her arms around herself as a cold breeze passes by. I take off my jacket and put it around her.

"Thank you."

I nod.

"I helped your father because...he's the father I have always dreamed to have."

Chapter 14. Misión Cumplida

It is times like this that I feel myself getting sad. Whenever I hear my father speak on the television, I feel unlucky that I have him as a father.

My eyes land on his gray expensive suit he's wearing as he gives his speech. He is a powerful surgeon and politician. He retired two years ago and dedicated the rest of his life to being a politician. He claims that he wants to do a lot of things to the people from charity to building homes, etcetera.

I don't believe shit.

If a father treats his daughter like some skunk living in his house, then I don't think he cares about the people.

"I don't understand how a father could do this," Victoria says as she looks at the screen in a disapproving look. She's someone who cares deeply about family and I could tell from only her being here for a few days.

Rafael's phone rings. He takes it out and answers the call.

"Yes, Alex?"

"Good. Destroy it."

When he hangs up, he opens his mouth to say something, but Cash turns up the volume of the TV and my father's voice blasts through the room.

"New evidence soon will be surfaced. These four criminals will be brought to justice and I promise you all, that I will not be biased at all. Here's to justice!" My father's voice is strong and powerful, making me feel a little bit uneasy.

"Not gonna happen. Cash and Alex found the book and destroyed it," Rafael says.

"What if he made other copies?" I ask anxiously.

"Ana, your father is a politician."

"So?"

He rolls his eyes and says, "He's not smart."

This makes me instantly laugh, making him smile a bit. Victoria and Manuel join me.

"Rafa, go to the warehouse and make sure all the shipments are going smoothly. I feel the men started to hold back after I came back," Manuel tells his son.

"Okay, father. There's also the deal with Roberto Sanchez. I will finish it with him today and start sending some shipments to his warehouse."

"Okay, son. Be careful."

When Victoria and Rafael left, I stayed behind to speak with Manuel. I was nervous to talk to him about this thing because I know he's a good person, but I just need to make sure of it. Besides, now that I am sitting in front of him, I became less nervous.

"Is there something bothering you, mi hija?" he asks as he sits on his chair, placing his arms on the table.

"Uncle...I just want to make sure that nothing...nothing illeg al...killing wise, is happening here."

"Let me worry about that, Ana."

"Look, I know all of us here are killers...but it triggers me."

"I promise you that you will not be hearing about anything killing-related in this house."

"Thank you, uncle."

I go to stand up and leave, but his firm voice stops me.

"Yes?"

"You know you can talk to me about anything, right?" he asks and I nod, giving him a warm smile.

"Thank you."

Cody and I are working on a research paper to submit to the medical institutions to suggest using better approaches when it comes to using some medical tools so they'd last longer.

I know...but don't blame me. It's one of Cody's obsessive goals.

"How about we make two samples so we see which one is better to submit?" Cody suggests.

"Cody, you're lucky I am even doing one," I say with a frown.

"Fine." He raises his arms in defense. "I am just so excited for this. Imagine if they found this helpful and used it?"

"Yeah, that would be amazing," I mumble.

"Oh, shut up!" He rolls his eyes playfully.

"So..." I start as I stop typing on my laptop. "How long have you been working here?" I ask, looking at him.

"When I finished university, I started working here.

"Oh, how did you meet with them?"

"Rafael and I are childhood friends. I was practically born here. His family and mine are close friends," he explains.

"Oh, I didn't know that." He hums.

"How did you meet with Manuel? I heard that you helped him escape, but why?" He asks this time.

"He needed a surgeon in prison and I performed a surgery on him. I was actually not practicing, but I couldn't let him die. It was either me or die on the way to the hospital," I replied, ignoring his second question as to why I helped him live.

"I see."

For the rest of the day, we kept working on our project. No one from the mafia came to check up or anything. It was only when Cody and I started to leave that the door were pushed open and Cash strolled in with Alex and Rafael.

Cash had a gunshot wound in his stomach, the blood oozing out of his body and into the floor.

Rafael had a few scratches and what possibly looked like a broken arm.

And Alex was holding Cash as he couldn't walk.

"Oh my god, what happened?" I exclaim, running toward them and grabbing Cash's arm to let him hold onto me.

"We were ambushed," Rafael replies.

"The same all black-clothed people?" Cody asks as he helps Cash lie on the operation table.

"Yes," Rafael replies.

"Ana, you take Rafael and I'll take Cash," Cody says and I nod.

I tell Rafael to lie down on the hospital bed while I check him up. He has a few scratches on his arm and his face. His lips are busted, but not too much. There's also a purple hue around his right eye. His left arm is one-hundred percent broken because just by looking at it, I want to look away.

It is severely broken.

I will need to perform a surgery.

I let him lie down on another operation table and give him anesthesia so he wouldn't feel anything.

I wear my gloves and mask, and start my work on his arm. I start to realign the broken bones. In order for it to stay in place during healing, I implant wires, some plates, and screws. I had to be very careful doing that even if it's a simple surgery for me.

When I finish, I throw the gloves and wear another pair. I then start working on the scratches, making sure they don't get infected. When I finish, I throw my gloves and close the curtain. I go to the other side of the room where Cody and Cash are.

"How's it going?"

"Not bad. The bullet didn't reach his liver, but it almost missed it. Want to help?

"Umm, I'd rather not," I reply, avoiding looking at Cash's body.

"It's okay, don't worry. The bullet is out and I am closing him up."

"Thank you, Cody."

In the next few hours, Rafael finally wakes up. He looks out of it as he stares at me like a lost puppy.

"What happened?" he mumbles enough for me to hear.

"This man..." Cody mumbles as he rearranges his desk. Cody has an OCD, obsessive compulsive disorder. His type is more into ordering and arranging stuff. I don't see there's a problem with that, he just likes his desk arranged and clean. He sometimes rearrange stuff in the same day, but he tries to control it.

"How are you feeling?" I ask Rafael as I help him get up. I don't want him to fall down from dizziness.

"I feel like shit. What the fuck did you do to me?" he asks playfully.

"I poisoned you, Rafael." A smirk makes its way to my lips.

He winks at me, making my heart thump. I blink in shock and confusion before I compose myself.

Before I leave the infirmary, Andrew walks in. I avoid looking at him because I still have negative feelings towards him. As I walk out of the door, Andrew grabs my arm and stops me.

"Ana, we need to talk."

Chapter 15. Honestidad

The way he's looking at me makes me think that he's scared to open his mouth and speak. In all the years I have spent with Andrew, he has never looked this nervous.

"There is nothing left to talk about, Andrew," I reply, snatching my arm and attempting to leave, but he yet again stops me.

"There's a lot of things to talk about, Ana. I have so many things that I want to say."

"Well, I don't."

"Ana, please," Andrew pleads.

Honestly, I would feel bad if I don't give him a chance to explain, but at the same, I don't think he deserves it.

"Just give me 5 minutes, please, Ana."

I sigh in defeat and nod, not wanting to be a bitch about it. It has been years after all and whenever he came to my parent's house to visit, I wouldn't be there. I cut him off when he disappeared for years before starting to visit a day or two yearly.

We walk to a room close to the infirmary and he closes the door behind him. He motions for me to sit, but I politely decline.

"Look, Ana, I know that you hate me right now. I disappeared when I went to university and trust me, I regret it. It's just... when I met Rafael and learned about his mafia, I had to join, and I didn't want any of you, especially you, to get involved. I was scared to visit because I didn't want our enemies to know my family. I changed my name and cut all ties with you all. I couldn't do that to you. Trust me, I tried coming more and tried to include you, but it was too risky, especially with Manuel's friend who betrayed him."

"Don't bullshit me, Andrew. Manuel's friend only betrayed them a year and a half ago, not twelve years ago."

"I know, I am not saying only for that reason...Ana please, just understand. You were the only one who got me despite being a sixteen-year-old kid," he pleads, grabbing my hands in his.

"You left me, Andrew. You left me despite knowing what he does. You know...you know how he hates me, how they hate me. I don't even know why they adopted me."

"Ana, I am so sorry. I never wanted to leave you, I swear. You will always be my sister and my favorite one. I failed you. I am so sorry, Hermana."

I look in confusion at him and was about to ask what he meant when he says, "sister."

"Every time I don't do a great job at the hospital, he gives me five whips on my back with his brown belt." I ignore everything he said and decide to share some of my memories with him. "It didn't happen frequently, the beatings, but the emotional abuse was constant. I was always reminded where I came from," I add, looking at his tearful eyes.

"Sarah became worse than before. Our mother forgot what compassion is like, but father was the worst."

"Ana, you do..."

"I want to," I cut his sentence and continue. "My only safe place was the hospital until I fucking killed the man who sexually assaulted me when I was walking down an alley bright in the morning, thinking nothing will happen because there were people around. But no one did shit when he grabbed my arm and took me despite my screams. Then I quit the hospital because I couldn't practice anymore. After all, the image of my hand holding the scalpel and damaging his organs couldn't leave my mind till today. Then I met my uncle at the prison where I was working as a general doctor. He became the father I never had and here I am, Andrew, in the place that you fucking wanted to protect me from. So, no, Andrew, your apology is not accepted."

By the end of my speech, Andrew's face is red, with tears running down as if they have been bottled up, waiting to be freed.

"I don't blame you for anything that happened, I only blame you for one thing and that is not being there when I needed you the most."

With that, I open the door and walk out, only to see Rafael with his broken arm, leaning on the wall in front of the door, with a blank expression on his face.

He heard everything.

I run to my room and lock the door. The guilt eats me as I think about what I said to Andrew. I can't bear feeling guilty for making someone else feel the same. It was like I told him that everything was his fault, which wasn't. Whatever happened to me, was not his fault. It's just that I have missed him and I never thought that one day he'd willingly leave me. I know he had, to protect me, but even then, I wasn't protected.

I look at my lifeless eyes. This only happens when I talk about something painful about my life. As much as I try to be strong and positive, at the end of the day, this is the real me.

A knock pulls me out of my trance. I walk to the door with lazy steps and a scowl. "Who is it?"

"It's me, darling," Victoria replies.

I unlock the door and pull it open.

"Are you okay? Andrew told me that you two talked and it wasn't good. Do you want to talk about it?"

"Not really, but is it okay if you stayed with me a little bit?"

"Sure, hun!"

She walks inside and sits on the bed, patting beside her for me to sit. I go and sit and then lean my head on her shoulder. "You know Victoria, you make me feel like I have a mother who cares about me."

"Oh, I am your mother. You can even call me mom," she replies, making me smile.

"What's the deal with you and uncle wanting me to call you both mom and dad?" I tease with a grin.

"Well, maybe because Alba had a twin sister but died while I was giving birth, so Manuel and I are too eager for you to call us that."

"Oh, I am sorry. What was her name?" I ask, looking at her now.

"Aliyah." She smiles. "We buried her near my mother."

"Well, I don't want to take her place or anything, but I'd love to call you mom."

"That'd be wonderful!" She squeals as she goes in for a hug.

A tight one might I add.

"By the way, lock me here because if I see Manuel or Rafael I would kill them."

"Why?" I giggle.

"Manuel because he sent our sons to get injured and Rafael for getting injured," she replies, shaking her head in disbelief. "Can you believe them?! They are stupid! I hate this," she adds, making me laugh.

"Don't worry about them, Rafael is good, just a broken arm, and Cash is okay."

"I know, but still. Cash is like a son to me and if anything happens to him, I'll burn this mafia down."

"Trust me, I'll help you with that."

"I knew choosing you as my daughter is the best choice!" She laughs.

"By the way, we are having a small party in two weeks for Rafael's birthday. Would you like to help me and Alba with the preparations?"

"Sure, I'd love to."

"Then, it's settled!" She claps her hands. "And by the way, don't ever hesitate to come to me when you need to talk, and please, I know it's none of my business, but give Andrew a chance, okay?"

"Thank you, mama, and I will."

Chapter 16. Pequenos Pasos

It's a week after the incident that broke Rafael's arm and damaged Cash's body. Alba and Victoria are preparing to throw a small birthday party for Rafael, who grumbles every time he hears about it. I am helping here and there whenever I finish my work at the infirmary. The amount of men this mafia has makes me think that half of the city is in it. Many women and men come to the infirmary for checkups, even if they already know that there's nothing wrong with them. Despite the infirmary situated in the main house where we all live, all the mafia men and women are welcomed whenever they want.

I take a quick shower and dry my hair. I put it up in a bun with my brown elastic and let two strands in the front down. I spray some perfume and put on lip balm.

I wear my two-piece black blouse, wide-leg pants, and black vans.

I walk out of my bedroom and head downstairs to eat breakfast with the rest. The sound of plates clattering travel to my ears as I walk down the stairs, feeling excited to eat Victoria's breakfast. She cooks amazing food.

"Good morning," I say as I walk into the kitchen. Victoria is standing behind the stove as usual, while two other maids helping around. Alba is cutting the lettuce as she looks to be in charge of the salad.

"Good morning, darling," Victoria replies with a smile.

"What should I do?" I ask, putting one of the two strands behind my ear.

"Don't do anything, honey. Just go and join Rafael in the dining room and look pretty."

Alba breaks out laughing, dropping the knife onto the table. My cheeks turn the color of roses and I avoid looking at either of them. The back of my neck feels hot, slowly spreading to the front. My heart beats accelerate, making me feel like I am about to faint.

"Oh, I am just kidding, no need to get all red," Victoria says with a smirk.

Damn it.

"I...I'll go t-then," I stutter, embarrassing myself even more.

I quickly leave the kitchen and head toward the dining room. Excitement spread through my body for no reason.

I am not excited to see Rafael, am I?

Cash, Alex, Andrew, and Rafael are sitting on the chairs talking as they wait for the food.

"Good morning," Andrew greets me as I walk in and join them.

"Good morning," I reply, looking at everyone. The rest replied with either good morning or hey.

The seats beside Andrew and Cash are empty, but I ignore Andrew and sit beside Cash, making his face fall.

"How are you, Cash?" I ask.

"Not bad, have been better," he replies with a teasing smile.

"And your arm, Rafael?" I direct my gaze at Rafael, who was already looking at me.

"Well, a good doctor fixed me up, so I am good," he replies, making me smile.

"Oh, don't boost my ego now."

He gives me a small smile as he scratches the back of his neck.

He's being nice...

The food started coming in. When everything was placed on the table, Victoria and Alba joined us, and Manuel joined after.

"Now that Rafael took over the mafia, how about we go on a trip, mi amor?" Manuel asks as he motions for us to start eating.

"Isn't it risky, honey?"

"Well, a little bit, but we will be using fake passports and we can easily transform our look. Besides, we could go to one of the neighboring islands."

"I don't mind, but when?"

"Whenever you want, mi amor," he replies.

"Okay. We can go after Rafael's birthday."

Rafael groans, his head buried in his hands. "Do you have to make me a birthday party?"

"Yes! What kind of question is that?" His mother scolds him. "You are going to be 31, Rafa. When will you get married and give me grandchildren?"

"God, not again," he mumbles enough for us to hear.

"I have been waiting for years, Rafa."

"Well, why not wait for more?" He arrogantly asks, making her face fall.

"Fine. It's your life anyways. Live it as you wish," she sadly replies.

"I am engaged, am I not? Because you both wanted this. But having kids was not part of the deal," he claps back.

As if on cue, Carmen walks in, her heels clicking on the tiles, making a loud noise. I could see Rafael's face fall once he saw her.

"Hola!" She greets me, kissing Manuel and Victoria on the cheek, and kissing Rafael on the lips, making my blood boil somehow. "I have missed you, mi amor."

He doesn't reply, earning a glare from her. She sits beside him on the chair and starts eating as if nothing happened.

"How's your father, Carmen?" Victoria asks.

"I don't know, haven't seen him in a week," Carmen replies nonchalantly.

Victoria's face turns into a confused one, hesitantly continues eating.

"Anyways, when will be the wedding, Rafael? I know it's a private matter, but my mother has been insisting on it," Carmen says, taking everyone aback by her sudden question, especially Rafael.

He looks at her and then at his father. I see Manuel looking intently at Rafael as if knowing what he is going to do. Rafael then looks back at Carmen, who's waiting for his response, and says, "There will be no wedding, Carmen."

"What?!" Carmen exclaims, standing up. "What do you mean there's no wedding?"

"Exactly what it means," he replies, taking out his ring and placing it in the palm of her hand.

"You can't do that, Rafa! Do you know what my father will do when he hears about this?"

"What?" He asks with a nonchalant attitude.

"The deal will be off and there will be war!" she replies, making him chuckle.

"I'll be here when that happens, now leave!"

She screams angrily and storms out of the house, leaving us all in shock.

Rafael is hardly breathing and his face is red from anger. He slams his fist on the table and leaves without saying a word. I look at Manuel, who is looking at Victoria, communicating silently. I then look at Rafael's friends, only to see them smiling.

"Finally," Cash exclaims happily.

"Rafa..." Alex warns.

"I can't believe Rafael ended it. I thought he was going to marry that wench." Alba's excited voice fills the room.

"Alba!" Victoria scolds, shaking her head. "What are we going to do, Manuelito?" She asks her husband.

"Well, we are not going to do anything. It's Rafael's problem now. why don't we talk about our vacation?" He smirks, making her turn all red as usual.

"Gosh, could you guys please do it somewhere else?" Alba shyly says.

I catch Cash looking dreamily at her, but she's oblivious to his stares...or acting as if she doesn't see them. Either way, he's screwed.

After breakfast, I find Rafael in the backyard, sitting on the bench by himself. I hesitate whether to go and talk to him or not, but eventually decide to.

"Are you okay?" I ask, sitting beside him.

"Yes, why wouldn't I be?"

"I know it was fake, but you just got out of a relationship."

"I don't care," he replies.

I place my hand on top of his and squeeze a little. He looks at me once I did that and gives me a small smile, squeezing back as if thanking me.

"I admit, I hated you at first, but now you don't seem that bad," he says, making me laugh.

"Well, I hated you too, though I was excited to meet uncle's son."

"What?" I ask when he kept looking at me with a different look I have never seen before.

"Nothing, I just never realized that your blue eyes have a brown tint before. They're beautiful."

My heart does its weird dance again and I get nervous. "Thank you..." I say, putting a strand of my hair behind my ear.

"Ana..."

"Yes?"

"Can I...Can I-"

"Rafa! Pablo's on the phone!" Alex interrupts.

"What does he want?"

"He seems mad and is demanding to talk to you, most probably about his daughter."

Chapter 17. Pesadillas

"What?" I press the phone to my ear.

"How dare you break up with my daughter!" His voice booms through the phone.

"We can't be together. Find another solution or don't. I don't care."

"You have just declared war on us, Rafael. Be ready." With that, he hangs up, making me slam the phone on the nearest wall in my office.

I don't care about fighting with him, my only concern is my father. I let him down and I couldn't push myself to stay with her. I am supposed to be with her forever, yet I couldn't stay with her for more than a month like a pussy. My emotions got the best of me and I acted according to my heart, something I can't bear to do. Mafia dons acting with their hearts will only result in their doom.

And I am not going to let that happen to me.

"Carmen knows where we live, we need to move," I tell Alex.

"What do you mean move? We can't just move like that."

"We can. We have many mansions across the country, choose one and let me know."

"Are you sure?"

"Yes, Alex."

I walk to my sister's room and knock on the door. She opens the door after a few seconds and glares at me.

"What do you want, Rafe?"

"Is it a bad time?"

"Yes! I am painting my nails. You can't just knock and disturb me."

I roll my eyes and walk in, making her yell at me to leave. "What the hell, Rafael?"

Oh, she used my full name. This is not good.

"I need your help with something."

She looks weirdly at me and says, "is it a girl problem again?"

"Yes," I reply hesitantly.

"What happened again?" She sighs, putting the nail polish away.

I sit on her bed beside her and start talking. "An hour ago, we were in the backyard and..."

"We as in who?" She cuts me off.

"You know who, Alba." I glare, making her giggle.

"Anyways, we were talking and she was making sure I was okay and..." I stop mid-sentence, scared to say the next words as I am embarrassed for an unknown reason. Maybe because I don't want to talk about this with my sister, but I have no one else to talk to, and I certainly won't talk about Ana to the guys.

"And what, Rafa?"

"I wanted to...kiss her."

"Good god, why do I have to listen to all of this!" She exclaims playfully.

"But I didn't! I was about to ask her but Alex cut me off."

"Well, good thing you have morals," she mumbles, picking up the nail polish again.

"But I am not finished!" I frown as she avoids me.

"Did something else happen?" She asks.

"No."

"Then you're finished."

"Alba..." I whine.

"If you want something, fucking get it before somebody else does."

"What do you mean?" I ask.

"Well, I do see Cody and Ana spending so much time together."

Anger arises as all I could feel and see is red. Ana and Cody? He wouldn't dare.

I storm out of the room and make my way to the infirmary. I push the door open only to see Ana and Cody sitting together and laughing. They seem taken aback by my visit and quickly stood up.

"Did something happen?" Cody asks.

"Follow me, Cody," I say firmly and walk out of the room.

I go to my office with him following me. My face is so red that Cody is avoiding looking at me, probably scared.

"Did I do something?" He hesitantly asks.

"Yes, yes you did."

"What?"

"Is there...is there something going on with you and Ana?"

"Ana? Of course, not. Why would you think that?"

"You seem cozy whenever I come to you."

"Rafa, did you forget that I am engaged?" He chuckles, covering his mouth with his hand.

"Didn't you say you broke up five months ago?"

"We got back together and I told you."

Fuck, I am stupid. Alba is stupid!

"Oh...okay."

"Rafa...do you like Ana?" He asks with a smile on his face.

"Me? Ana?..." I chuckle, "...of course, not."

"Oh, too bad."

"What's too bad?" I ask.

"She talks about you a lot that someone would think you two have something going on."

"She does?"

"Mhmm...now if there are no more accusations, I'd like to go back to work."

"Sorry," I say, scratching the back of my neck.

He smiles at me, shakes his head, and leaves.

Fuck, she talks about me...what does she say? I should have asked.

I go to the living room and see my mother sitting on the couch, drinking tea.

"Hey."

"Hola, honey."

"Can we talk?"

"Of course," she replies, placing the tea on the table. "Tell me, honey."

"Are you mad at me? For breaking up with Carmen?"

She gasps dramatically and says, "of course, not. I didn't even like her. I admit, she was good for business, but that's it. Besides, I want you to choose someone that you want and I apologize for forcing you to get engaged with Carmen."

"It's okay...you don't have to apologize. It's just...my priorities have changed."

"Does that mean you like another girl?" She smirks, making me roll my eyes.

"No, mom."

"Mhm, anyways, tomorrow is your party, how do you feel?"

"Can we not do it?"

"We are doing it, Rafa!" She glares, making me shut my mouth.

"Fine."

The next day arrives and I could sense that it was going to be a disaster, mostly because it is my birthday and my mother insists on giving me the party of my life. The party will be small, and only close family members are allowed. I am sure my uncle from my mother's side will come along with his wife and two daughters whom I love. One is fifteen and the other is twelve.

He's my mother's younger brother.

I take a shower and wear my outfit for today. I wear a black suit, wanting to get it over with and not change later for the party. I comb my hair and style it how I like it. I spray perfume and walk out of the room.

The first person I see is Ana, right in front of my bedroom do or...in a towel wrapped around her body. A little short towel.

The air is knocked off of my chest.

"G-Good morning," I say, trying hard not to stutter.

"Hey...sorry, I'm...I wanted to bring something from Alba's room."

"It's okay..."

This is awkward. How could I tell her that I want to ravish her right now but that I can't?

She nods and walks fast to Alba's room, shutting the door behind her.

I try to breathe in and out to get some oxygen back into my body.

I walk downstairs, not wanting to stay outside of my bedroom door, looking like a fool.

I find my mother cooking in the kitchen, not letting anyone touch anything.

"Morning."

"Buenos Dias, son," she replies.

"What are you doing?"

"Food for the party," she replies.

"Mom, you know you don't have to do all this."

"Really? Then who'll do this if it's not your mother?"

"We didn't have to do anything of this at all."

"Bullshit!" She sneers. "This is your 31st birthday and it has to be special."

"Why?"

"Because it is the year that you will find love."

"And how do you know that?"

"Oh, honey, everyone in this house saw how you look at Ana, we are not stupid."

I quickly cover her mouth just in time that my sister and Ana to walk in. I look like I have been caught saying something wrong and I hope Ana didn't hear anything.

"What's going on?" Alba asks.

"Nothing!" I quickly reply, giving my mother a side glare as if telling her not to say anything.

"Nothing, darling. How are you?"

"I am good, mama," Alba replies, kissing her on the cheek.

"And what about you, Ana?" My mother asks.

"I am good, thank you."

Ana's cheeks are red and she looks extremely shy for the first time. She was never this shy.

"You okay?" I ask when I stood near her.

"Yes, everything's okay," she replies with a smile. She puts a strand of her front behind her ear, an act she often does whenever she's with me.

Is she shy because I am here?

I grin like a stupid man thinking about it and earn a weird, questioning look from my sister.

"Anyways, your uncle Arturo is coming today with Camila and the kids." My mother's voice snaps me out of my daydream.

Alba and just shrug. I already knew and I am sure Alba did too.

In the evening, uncle Arturo came and we all gathered in the backyard, along with Cash, Alex, and Cody. Cody's fiancée also came.

"Happy birthday, son," uncle Arturo says, hugging me. Camila, his wife, wishes me a good year and gives me a gift.

The girls, Alma and Alicia, gave me a hug that lasted about ten minutes.

Nah, just kidding.

"Rafael," Ana calls.

"Yes?"

"Can we talk a little bit inside?" She asks, pointing at the house.

"Sure."

We walk inside and upstairs to her room. She tells me to come in and goes to bring something from her wardrobe.

"This is for you," she gives me a small bag.

"Oh, you didn't have to," I say, opening the bag and taking out the silver bracelet, and putting it on.

"I love it, thank you," I say, hugging her.

She seems taken aback by my sudden hug but hugs me back.

"It's nothing."

"How did you even get it?"

"Cody. I told him to send me photos and I chose one."

"Thanks again." I smile and I hesitate whether to kiss her on the cheek or not, but I decided to go for it.

I lean in and kiss her cheek. Her face is hot and the breath intake she took makes me think that I affect her.

She gives me a timid smile, showing off her dimples that I have never seen before.

She stays frozen in her place as if waiting for me to do something else, but I don't. I want to take it slow as much as I could. She's too precious that I don't want to rush things. Besides, I still have to have a conversation with my father because Ana is so important to him and I know what he might think. I just need to sort my stuff first before going into anything.

Chapter 18. Culpa

It is the week after my birthday party. I am still wearing the bracelet Ana gave me. It feels illegal to take it off and I don't want to.

I am at the warehouse, working with my men to find Storm. He doesn't even deserve to be called uncle anymore. This warehouse is 30 minutes away from the house. This is the place where all of my men reside and work. The house, however, is where we live and get healed in. My mother made sure that the infirmary remains at the house, but we made sure to have a small one at the warehouse just in case we couldn't reach the villa.

"Boss! Someone left a package at the door!" One of my men, Angel, yells. I quickly stand up and run downstairs to make sure it isn't a bomb. Jeremy, our bomb analyzer, comes with me to check the package.

It's a square brown box, taped from all the holes. No one touches the box as Jeremy and I walk toward it and analyze it.

"Everybody move back!" I yell.

The men listen and step away from the package. The atmosphere suddenly shifts as Jeremy opens the package, but no one was ready for what we're about to see.

A head.

Not just any head. The mafia's hacker's head, Justin.

Jeremy steps back and vomits on the floor. Everyone starts gagging at the scene, but I only stared at the head of the nineteen-year-old boy. He was just a boy, who was doing his job. The one I ordered him to do.

Today was his off day. His day to spend with his family.

Guilt fills my body as I continue to stare at his face. He died because of me, because I couldn't protect him and because I employed a young boy for his talents.

What am I going to tell his parents?

"Rafa..."

"Rafa!"

"Rafael!" Cash's voice pulls me out of my depressing thoughts.

I look at him, he looks very concerned.

"Are you okay, brother?" he asks, kneeling to my level and grabbing my shoulder with his right hand.

I don't answer because I am not.

"It's not your fault, Rafa."

I look at him this time and say, "It is."

"It isn't. Don't let his death convince you that you killed him. We are the mafia, things like this are bound to happen," he explains, trying to convince me.

"I promised that I'd protect him."

"And you did, this whole year, you did. But you can't protect him forever."

"His parents...what am I going to tell them?" I ask, standing up.

"I don't know, man, but I will be there with you."

My eyes betray me for the first time in front of my men as a single tear drops from my eye and onto my cheek. I quickly wipe it off and walk to my office. Alex and Cash don't follow me, knowing that I need some time to myself.

I reach my office and take out my inhaler from the drawer. I only use it whenever I get a panic attack or feel sad. It helps sometimes.

Justin Moralo...a name I will forever remember.

I grab my keys and leave the warehouse. I know who did this. It's Storm. He has to be the one because Justin was looking into his system the day before he was murdered, which was yesterday.

I drive to the house and park my car. I step out and stroll inside. My mother, Alba, and Ana are sitting in the living room, drinking alcohol, bright in the morning.

What has gotten into them?

"Brother! Welcome home!" Alba slurs, causing Ana and my mother to giggle.

When they see my face, they immediately sober up. Alba and my mother have a concerned faces and Ana has a confused one.

"What happened?" My mother asks, putting the glass on the table.

"Nothing. I will be in my room," I reply, leaving them to have fun.

They are better off not knowing anything, especially when they might have a lot on their plates.

I walk to my father's office and enter. Andrew's face comes into view as I walk further inside. My father is the first to see me and he immediately stands up. "Son, I heard about what happened, are you okay?" He asks, grabbing Andrew's attention.

"Yes, why wouldn't I be?" I reply nonchalantly.

"Andrew, leave us alone," my father orders, earning a nod from Andrew. He stands up and leaves, but not before tapping my shoulder.

When the door closes, my father motions for me to sit. He looks determined to know how I feel, but I won't say anything. The only person to who I feel like I could open myself is my sister and right now, she is not in the right state of her mind.

"Son, Cash filled me on everything. It's not your fault."

"Dad, I don't want to talk about it. Let's talk about Storm. He did this and we can't waste any more time in finding him."

"We will, I promise. Andrew has got some leads in this case. He found out that Storm might be hiding somewhere in Italy."

"Italy, why there?" I ask in confusion.

"Because he knows that we'll never go there."

"Why don't we prove him wrong?"

"It's dangerous and you know it."

"He's getting to us even when he's in Italy, we have to do something."

"And we will, but we need a plan. A good one."

"What are you suggesting?" I ask, crossing my legs together. I run a hand through my hair as a yawn escapes my lips.

Not the right time.

"A plan like the one we did back in Vancouver when we escaped Ana's house."

"You want me to play house again?" I chuckle, not minding the idea. I'd love to do anything with Ana, especially playing house.

"You don't seem to mind like before," he smirks, making me roll my eyes.

"Actually, there's something I want to talk to you about."

"Tell me."

"I know now is not the time, especially after Justin's death, but I want to talk to you now because I know I won't later. It's about Ana."

"What about her? Did something happen?" He asked with concern.

"Nothing happened, dad. It's just...I want to ask for your permission because I know you care deeply about her."

"Permission for what?"

"Permission to...love her?" It came out as a question, but he understood immediately because the glare he gave me...says it all.

"Love her? You like her? You? Like a girl?"

"What do you mean?" It was my turn to glare.

"Son, I thought I'd never see this day ever. I thought you could love Carmen, but it didn't happen, and then I thought that you just are not capable of love."

"But I love my family," I say in confusion.

"Loving your family is different. Anyways, Ana is very special to me, are you sure of your feelings?"

"Yes, dad. I have never felt like this before."

"Good. Because if you hurt her, I will cut your balls off."

"Thanks," I grin as he chuckles.

My thoughts immediately shift to Justin as if it's a switch. My mood changes and sadness washes over me.

I excuse myself and go to my room. If I don't sleep, I will keep thinking about him.

I lay on the bed, still wearing my outfit and shoes. I just don't have the energy to change. However, I only take off my shirt, leaving my chest bare.

I close my eyes to sleep when a knock makes me jerk up.

"Come in!"

The door opens and a drunk Ana walks in. Her hooded eyes look lustily at me as she walks my way.

Who fucking drinks early in the morning?

"Are you drunk?" I ask and she smiles.

"Yes, how did you know?" She slurs, making me grin.

She sits on the bed and all of a sudden straddles me.

"A-Ana?" My voice shakes as she starts moving. She circles her arm around my neck and leans in.

"You know, you look so hot right now."

"Ana, you're drunk."

"Who cares, I just want to forget."

"Forget what? Tell me." My voice softens as the smile on her face is replaced by a frown.

"I want to forget him."

A sudden feeling of jealousy rises inside of me as I listen to her.

"Who? Forget who, Ana?" My voice hardens.

"Don't yell at me!" She starts crying.

"I didn't yell, Ana," I gently say as I caress her cheeks.

"Okay...thank you."

God, she's so drunk.

"I want to forget him, the man I killed. Can you help me forget?"

"I can...come here," I say, opening my arms for her to hug me.

"Can I get a kiss here like last week?" She asks, pointing at her cheek.

I grin and nod. I kiss her on the cheek, making her moan.

Suddenly, she falls asleep, in my arms, and on my lap.

Chapter 19. Desastre

Opening my eyes, the first thing I see is a chest. A man's chest. More specifically, Rafael's bare chest. I cross my eyebrows in confusion as to how I, or we, ended up in this position. But then all the memories of a few hours ago come crashing down on me, making me widen my eyes in horror as the realization of what I had done hit me.

I quickly jerk up, not caring if he wakes up. My ears and cheeks become hot and red as shyness washes over me. My eyes could not leave his figure as he sleeps soundly on the bed.

A sudden urge to cuddle with him hit me like a brick, and all of a sudden, my body falls again against his. I wrap my arms around his body and place my head on his shoulder, and close my eyes as if I hadn't been up for a minute ogling him. He shifts a little but doesn't wake up, not that I checked. I open my eyes to check if he woke up only to meet with his. A smirk stretches on his face as he sees me looking at him.

Another wave of shyness hit me as I begin to retract my arms, but he stops me with his hands, placing them back around him. I adjust my head on his shoulder while still looking at him.

"Hey..." he says, grabbing my waist and pushing my closer to his chest. I don't know what game he's playing, but I fucking love it. It's weird to think that all of a sudden, we became this things that doesn't have a name. Sometimes he teases and sometimes I do. Sometimes he flirts and sometimes I do.

"Hi." I squeak.

"Are you okay or does your head hurt?" he asks and I immediately realize that my head had been hurting, but I was too busy being shy and ogling him to notice.

I flinch as I place my hand on my head and massage it.

"It hurts."

"Of course, it does. I am surprised you're not puking."

"Shut-up," I reply, squinting my eyes at him.

"So, do you remember what you did before you fell asleep?" he asks, making me instantly red. I unwrap my arms and this time, he allows me. I sit up and look at him with a shy look.

"Yes...I am sorry."

"You don't have to apologize. I thoroughly enjoyed it."

I glare at him and hit his arm. "It will never happen again because I am never drinking."

"Who said you'll have to drink to do it again?" he says with a smirk.

"In your dreams!" I say with a proud look.

"Oh, in my dreams, we have done so much more."

"Pervert." I comment as I step out of the bed.

"Where're you going?" He asks, halting my movements to open the door.

"My room. I need to freshen up before going for dinner."

"Don't you want one of my kisses?" He grins, making me roll my eyes.

"Shut up!" I groan, opening the door and stepping out of his room.

A smile stretches on my face once I am out of his sight as I recall what he said.

I walk into my room and change my clothes. I wear a pair of denim high-waisted jeans pairing it up with a green sleeveless shirt. I go to the bathroom and brush my teeth. I then remove my makeup and apply it again. I put my hair up in a ponytail and wear butterfly earrings.

After spraying some perfume, I make my way downstairs. The house is in an unusual silence. Every evening, there has to be some noise around the house, mainly from Cash, who cracks jokes here and there. So, not hearing his voice came as a big surprise to me. The only reason he wouldn't be here is if he's on a mission.

When I reach the living room, Victoria, Manuel, and Andrew come into view. I furrow my eyebrows as I see them engaged in a serious conversation.

"Good evening," I greet, stopping their talk.

"Good evening, honey," Victoria smirks.

"Good evening," Manuel and Andrew reply.

"Where is everyone?" I ask as I sit beside Victoria.

"Cash and Alex are at the warehouse. Alba is out with her friends. And Rafael...well, you know where he is, don't you?" Victoria says, making my cheeks hot and red.

"Don't make her shy, baby," Manuel says, making her giggle.

"Have I missed something?" Andrew asks.

"It's none of your business," I quickly reply before anyone says anything. His face falls and a sudden regret comes over me.

"Anyways, Ana, Andrew found out that your father is missing," Manuel starts.

"Missing, how?" I ask.

"I don't know, but our mother called me and she told me that he hasn't shown up in a week. He's also not answering his calls."

"Wow, I didn't see this coming," I reply.

"What if someone has done something to him?" Andrew asks.

"So? Besides, I am sure nothing has happened to him."

"You don't get it. If something happened to him, the media and the police might think you did it. After all, he has been going on TV nonstop, talking shit about you."

Shit.

"You're right. What are we going to do?" I ask, looking at my uncle.

"We must find him."

My father is a very smart man. If he doesn't want to be found, he won't be. He knows what he's doing and he would do anything for the police to get me, even if he has to fake his death. But what if something really happened to him? What if someone kidnapped him for something that he did to them? I won't be surprised if he did something bad to someone. After all, he didn't reach the top by working hard.

"Honestly, now that I think about it, I don't care. Whether he's okay or not, I don't care. Whether they put the blame on me or not, I don't care," I say, taking them aback. "Besides, there isn't any proof that I am involved in his disappearance."

As if on cue, the doorbell rings and the housekeeper runs to open the door. All of us were expecting Alba to waltz into the house but to our surprise, two police officers stood behind the door.

"We're here to speak with Lilia James."

That's Victoria's fake name.

Shit.

Chapter 20. Almost Busted

ANA

"We're here to speak with Lilia James." One of the officers says. We are sitting in the living room and there's no way any of the officers could see us.

Victoria stood up and walked to the door with confidence. There's no way the police could know that Victoria is Manuel's wife, or that she has kids.

"Yes?" We hear her ask as she stands in front of them.

"Ms. James, we are very sorry to disturb you at this time, but we have been requested to visit you and inform you that there are very high-profile criminals hiding in Burnaby. Just be careful and keep your doors closed."

"Thank you so much for informing me. I will be leaving the country soon, and I hope you catch them soon," Victoria replies with much emotion.

"Thank you, Ms."

With that, they left. Victoria comes back feeling relieved that we weren't caught.

"It's not long before they find you here. We need to move as soon as possible," Victoria says before gulping the glass of water in one go.

"Where do we fucking move?" Rafael asks.

No one comes up with any suggestions so I blurt out the riskiest option out there. "Mexico."

"Mexico?" Andrew asks in confusion.

"Why Mexico?" Manuel asks.

"I have a house there, bought it when I moved out from home," I explain.

"Why did you buy one?" Andrew's curious voice speaks.

I look nervously at everyone. "I wanted to escape there."

"It's too risky. The house is under your name." Rafael says.

"Not really. I bought it with a fake ID because I didn't want my father to find out. You could say I got it illegally."

"How did you manage that? Who helped you?" Andrew asks, looking confused as hell.

I huff before saying, "I have a friend, Mia Gonzalez. Her father is in the mafia. They helped me."

"Demetrio Gonzalez..." Manuel speaks up as he looks deep in thought.

"Yeah, you know him?" I ask.

"We used to be friends, but stopped when I moved here."

I nod. The atmosphere of the room shifts and a sudden tension envelops us. I didn't know that talking about them would get my uncle and the rest in such a mood.

"How do you even know these people?" Andrew asks as if he is scolding me and cares about my protection.

"Mia went to university with me. Besides, why do you care?"

"Of course, I care!" he exclaims, making my anger flare up.

"You don't get to say that now! If you really cared, you wouldn't have left! You're such a hypocrite."

Pain washes over his features, making me feel instantly bad. I don't like to make anyone feel sad because of me, but I just couldn't hold it back. I tried to act nice and forgive him, but it was just not that easy. Forgiveness is crucial in every relationship, but what he did is too much for me to handle. I have waited for him...for so many days, months, and years. He never came. He only came on holiday's, but I was too hurt to see him. It was as if he came out of petty.

I ran out of the living room and went to my bedroom. I happen to do that whenever Andrew is involved in any argument. He's just making me so mad and I don't know what to do with him anymore.

ANDREW

"I don't know what to do anymore. I have tried everything," I say as I look at my hands, too embarrassed to look at anyone's face.

Silence fills the living room as no one speaks up. I know that they don't know what to say as well, but I would appreciate it if someone said anything, even if it's to scold me. This family means everything to me. I never thought that one day I'd say this, but it means more to me than my real family. They took me in despite everything. Despite who my father is.

"I am sure she'll come around, honey. Just give her time," Victoria says gently. "One time Rafa stopped talking to me because I practically forced him to meet this girl, who later on became obsessed with him that she followed him everywhere. He didn't talk to me for a whole month. It was torture."

"That's different. I abandoned my sister...for years. I didn't even call her. I was her hero and I dumped her like she was nothing."

"But you did that for a reason, no?" Manuel points out.

"Si, I wanted to protect her. But now I realized that I protected her from the wrong people as the person who hurt her was living with her all this time."

"What's done is done, man. Don't revisit the past. Focus on how you'll make her forgive you," Rafael says, tapping my shoulder.

"You know what hurts, Rafa? Is that I knew what kind of a father mine was, yet I left her," I reply, shaking my head. "She'll never forgive me."

"I don't want to speak instead of her, but I am sure she will forgive you. She loves you so much, that's why she is hurt. She didn't expect you to do that because she trusted you. But she will understand that you did that to protect her from bad people."

"But here she is, Rafa...in the place that I wanted to protect her from, just like she said."

Rafael gives me a side hug as Victoria joins. Manuel sat there awkwardly because everyone knew he doesn't hug.

He only hugs his wife.

The front door opens and Alba walks in.

"What's going on? Why the atmosphere here sucks?" She asks, crossing her eyebrows.

"A lot has happened since you left. Pack your bags, we're moving," Manuel tells his daughter.

"Moving?!" Alba shrieks. "Where?"

"Mexico."

Before she could say anything, Cash and Alex kick the door open and walk in.

"I can't move! All my friends are here...hell, my boyfriend is here!"

"Boyfriend?!" Rafa, Manuel, Cash, and I shriek.

"I-I mean...a guy friend."

"Who is here?" Cash suddenly questions, making us all confused. But I immediately knew that he has a thing for her because his fiery eyes cannot be mistaken for anything else.

"What is it to you!" she claps back, glaring at him.

"Alba!" Rafael's voice booms through the living room. "Who the fuck is this guy? What's his name?"

"Daddy, tell them!" Alba runs to her father and hugs him.

"Boys! It is none of your business! I will deal with it! Now pack your bags!" Manuel exclaims, making Alba smirk in victory.

Chapter 21. Cash Is Screwed

Moving is never easy. I despise it. I hate it.

I have been moving all my life from one city to another, from one house to another, and sometimes, from one country to another. It has been Alex's and mine life. But I am grateful as much as I hate it.

And you know what the worst part is? That I'll move wherever just to be close to her.

My Alba.

"Cash, take this box and put it in Alba's room," Victoria tells me, making me feel all giddy on the inside.

At least she trusts me to be near her daughter.

We moved this morning to Ibiza, an island in Spain. This is the only place that we could think of where the police won't search for a while, especially when this island is full of gangsters. It's really not safe to be here either, but since we are the Spanish mafia, everyone was expecting us and gave in to our orders.

I pick up the heavy box and march toward Alba's room. I see her organizing her clothes in her closet, oblivious to my presence. I stand there like an idiot and look at her like a creep. It wasn't until the box fell from my hand that I came back to my senses.

"Cash! You scared the shit out of me, you asshole!" She yells, walking my way and hitting me in the arm.

"Sorry! It's heavy, what did you put in it?"

"It's none of your business!" She yells in frustration, making me grin.

"They are your medals, aren't they," I tease, making her groan. "I don't understand why you're embarrassed."

"I am not embarrassed, I am just...just shut up!"

I hold my arms up in surrender as my grin grows. As much as she seems to despise me and always yells at me, I just happen to fall in love with her more if that's even possible.

"Why are you still standing here? Go."

"Okay...sorry," I say and turn around to leave.

"Cash, wait!"

"Yes?" I gently ask as I look into her mesmerizing eyes.

"I...I didn't mean to yell, sorry."

"It's okay." I smile, earning one back.

I go back to the front of the house to help the rest with moving the stuff in. I see Manuel and Victoria loading stuff inside, as well as, a few of Rafael's men. Rafael and Ana are moving stuff inside too. I go and help Victoria and Manuel because as much as they love me, I need them to love me more, just in case a miracle happens and Alba likes me back.

Nothing is impossible, right?

"Cash, take this to the kitchen," Victoria tells me and I immediately nod.

Victoria doesn't like movers...or Manuel's men to move things in. He had spent hours trying to convince her of letting him bring two of his men...well, Rafael's men now.

She believes that they will break her stuff, which she isn't wrong about.

A loud noise stops my movements. I walk out and see one of Rafael's men kneeling before a vase he was loading inside. Victoria is standing in front of him with her jaw on the floor and her arms crossed over one another.

She doesn't say anything to the poor man, but to Manuel...he is officially screwed. She motions for him to follow her with her eyes, and he obliges.

I load the rest of the stuff inside and send the men back to the warehouse. I take the deceased vase and pick up all the pieces from the ground. I bring super glue and try to fix it. I sit on the ground in front of the door and start gluing the pieces together, hoping it would work. Manuel and Victoria are nowhere to be seen.

"What are you doing?" Ana asks.

"Putting this back together."

"Do you need my help?" she asks.

"No, thanks."

"Do you need Alba's help then?" she asks and I look up at her only to see a smirk on her lips. "Don't worry, I know."

"You know?! How do you know? Who also knows?" I fire questions at her, leaving the task on hold.

"Relax, no one knows, but me."

"How?"

"You're really that obvious, Cash."

"Oh my god, if Rafael knows he'll kill me. Don't tell him!" I start to panic.

"Why would he kill you?" she asks, kneeling to my level.

"He's overprotective over her..." I reply.

"Doesn't mean he'll kill you," she retorts.

"Just don't tell him, please."

She sighs and replies, "Don't worry, Cash, I won't."

I quickly finish the vase and carefully take it inside Victoria to see. Maybe seeing the vase alive again would make her forgive Manuel.

I find her sitting in the living alone. I wonder where Manuel is.

I remember the day Victoria and Manuel took Alex and me in. We were just kids back then and they treated us like family. I remember Manuel and young Rafael found us in an alley, sleeping. Rafael was very young back then and he was the one who found us when he was with his father visiting some people. Our parents abandoned us at a very young age and I don't remember any of them now. Victoria and Manuel have always been my family to the point that I used to call them mom and dad. They didn't really adopt us, but they took care of us. But I now feel weird calling them mom and dad because that would make me feel like I am related to Alba and I don't want that.

"Oh my god, what have you done?" Victoria gasps as she sees the vase in my hand.

"I don't know if it'll stay intact, but I hope so," I nervously say, handing the vase over to her. She takes it from me and smiles. "Oh, honey, you didn't have to do that, but I really appreciate it. Thank you."

She hugs me just in time as Alba comes to the living room.

"What did he do to win one of your lovely hugs?" Alba asks, making me chuckle.

"He super-glued the vase that fell," Victoria says, making Alba widen her eyes.

"Anyways, I have to go," I say.

"Okay, honey. Don't forget dinner today."

I nod and leave but not before stealing a glance at Alba, who was already looking at me with a soft look. This is the first time that she doesn't glare at me. Even when we were younger, she used to hit me a lot even though I was older. But I never hit her back, not because she was a girl or anything, but because I was scared of her...still am.

She has this fire within her that burns everyone along the way, especially guys who get close to her. I don't know if she was ever in a relationship before, but I doubt it.

I go to the backyard and find Rafael standing with Alex. When they see me come, they stop talking and just look at me.

"Hey...what are you guys doing?"

"Nothing, just talking about work. Where were you?" Alex asks.

"Helping Victoria with some things, just finished."

"You have been trying so hard to please my mother these days, why?" Rafael asks as he narrows his eyes.

"Nothing, I just...she's like a mother to me, you know?"

"Yeah, but you have been extra helpful," he insists.

"It's nothing, really..."

Rafael nods and doesn't say anything else, but Alex stares at me as if he knows why I was making my relationship better with Victoria, even though it has always been good. She's like my mother after all. Well, better than my mother.

"Anyways, how about we do something fun?" Alex suggests.

"Like what?" Rafael asks.

"Like going to a club kind of fun."

"Now? While we're in the middle of getting caught by the police and killed by the enemies?" Rafael asks.

"Uh...yes."

"Great, I am in."

Chapter 22. Intimacy

Instead of going to the club, we decided to go to the park. I know, a 180-degree change. That was honestly Alba's idea.

So here we are now, sitting in a circle in the middle of the dark park, with no light coming from anywhere other than the flashes coming from our phones. It's a good thing actually, that there's no light because we are fugitives, at least everyone is except Alba and Andrew, who is sitting next to Alba and getting glares from poor Cash.

I guess I should have phrased that better.

While Cash is too busy glaring at Andrew, Andrew is busy staring at Alba. She's talking to her brother, ignoring both men, who are sitting beside her. After apparently having enough of them, she opens a conversation that would make both of them suffer from anger.

"Rafa, there's something I have been meaning to talk to you about."

"What is it, Alba?" Rafael asks as he scrolls through his phone.

"I...remember Jeremy? The guy I had been talking to the last few months?"

"I don't remember a Jeremy, but what's up?" he asks, putting his phone aside. "Did he do something to you?"

"No, no! He did nothing. It's just...we started dating last month."

Silence fills the air as the three men sitting with us look at Alba with angry looks. I didn't even know Andrew has a thing for Alba, but apparently, he does.

"What do you mean, you started dating?" Rafael asks in a deep voice, making me want to place my hand on his arm to stop him from any advances.

"What it exactly means...I guess," she replies nervously.

"Have you been meeting with him?" he asks.

"No, he does not live in Spain. He's in the U.S."

"How did you meet him?"

"He came here a couple of months ago to visit and we met."

"Where?"

"Rafa, can you stop the investigation already." Alba huffs, earning a glare from her brother.

"Answer me, Alba."

"At the bar."

"Are you serious?! You met with a guy at a bar and now you are dating?" he gets worked up and his tone becomes harsher.

I finally decide to place my hand on his arm, making him look at me. I mouth a "calm down" to him, and he immediately calms down as if remembering I am still here.

It makes my heart warm knowing that I have a certain effect on him just as he has on me. A blush makes its way to my cheeks, taking me away from the scene unfolding in front of me. Rafael and I have been getting close to one another and it's something I thought would never happen, seeing that I hated him when I first met him. He was arrogant and rude and still is, but now it's different. Now, I like him.

"Rafa, please..." Alba's voice cracks as a tear threatened to fall from her gorgeous eye.

Rafael sighs and doesn't say anything. He looks at me as if trying to calm himself down before turning back to her and saying, "Fine. If he makes you happy, then I am happy."

"Really?!" Alba and Cash say at the same time.

"What is it to you?" Alba asks Cash in a harsh manner.

"Nothing..." he mumbles, his face falling to the ground, not meeting her eyes.

I could see from the corner of my eye that Rafael is looking at Cash in confusion, probably putting the pieces together. When I see his mouth a little open as he looks at Cash, I feel certain that he now knows that his best friend likes his sister.

And from what I gathered these past few months, Rafael would rather let his best friend dating his sister than a stranger he knows nothing about.

"Anyways, let's play something," Alex changes the subject, startling us because he hasn't said anything since we came.

"Dude, make some noise next time," Andrew glares at Alex.

"Sorry..."

I get a little bit closer to Rafael without him noticing. For some reason, I feel like I want to be near him all the time, especially when I don't see him for hours.

My thigh touches his, making him turn and look at me. I don't look at him because of my shyness, but what he does next makes my stomach flutter.

He sneaks his arm around my waist and squeezes a little bit, pushing me more toward him. No one sees what's going on as the flashlights from our phones don't capture our bodies, only faces.

My heart beats very fast against my ribcage, making me almost faint from excitement. It doesn't remove his arm the whole time and only moves his fingers in a circular motion, drawing circles.

He then gets close to my ear and murmurs words that made me almost wet my pants. "Leave your door open tonight. I am coming to your room if that's okay."

I shyly nod and smile, looking into his amused eyes. I don't trust the words that would come out of my mouth right now.

"I am bored...and single," Alex says, seeing that no one listened to his game suggestion.

"Is Alex drunk? He has never been this talkative," I whisper to Rafael, who chuckles.

"He is."

"Let's just go," Alba says, standing up.

Cash is the first to stand up after her and then followed by everyone else. I could see Cash's sad face even in the night and I feel for him. He has been nothing but gentle and kind. I know she cannot control the way she feels about someone, but I hope she really sees him. And I feel she would only see him when she losses him.

We all drive back home. Victoria and Manuel are asleep as we entered the mansion. The lights are off and the only thing that could be heard is the wind from behind the windows.

I go to my room and excitement spreads through my body as I recall what Rafael told me. He'll be coming to my room tonight and I am very nervous. What would he want to do? Would he just want to talk or do something else? And what would he want to do if not talk?

I change into my only available pajamas, the ones that I am embarrassed to wear in front of anyone. That's just my luck for today.

Cat-printed pajamas. Long sleeves and shorts.

I sit on my bed and wait impatiently for the door to be opened and for Rafael to walk in. I look at the clock and it reads 2:02 AM.

After ten minutes, at 2:12 AM, my bedroom door is pushed open and Rafael walks in, trying so hard not to make a sound. I look at him and try so hard to suppress my giggle that was making its way out.

He sits beside me on the bed, way too close to me. "Hey," he says with a grin.

"Hi..." I shyly say, tucking a strand of hair behind my ear.

"So..."

"So..."

"You know, you're making it so hard for me."

"What do you mean?" I ask in confusion.

He leans in until his nose hit mine as a smile plays on his lips. "How do you expect me not to kiss those lips whenever I see you..."

"What's preventing you?" I say with confidence, immediately feeling embarrassed, but I don't show it.

"That's exactly why I am here, to tell you that there's nothing that's going to prevent me from doing this," he says and slams his lips onto mine in a mind-blowing deep kiss.

Our lips fight against each other as both of us fight for dominance. He sneaks his arms around my waist, making me squeal at the sudden contact. This gives him the gateway to insert his tongue and deepen the kiss. He pulls me until I straddle him, my bottom part against his. I moan into the kiss making him groan in return.

When we break apart, we look into each other's eyes, getting lost in each other.

"Why haven't we done this before?" he asks, eyeing my lips.

"I don't know... I wish we have done it sooner."

"Me too."

He captures my lips again and this time starts grinding. I couldn't stop the moan that came out, making him smirk knowing that he is affecting me.

He takes my pajama top off without breaking the kiss. His fingers pull my bra straps down and then trail kisses from my jaw down my neck.

"Rafa..."

"Fuck, call me that again."

"Rafa."

Chapter 23. Finding Truth pt. 1

Rafael

I hum as I listen to what she is saying. She is telling me about her late dog, Doug, who played a big role in protecting her from her abusive father. I did not know that she lived in abuse to this extent. Her father is an ass and I will do everything in my power to find him and hand him to the authorities. I will also do everything in my power to clear my father's name. I want us to live a normal life, and be able to go out without fearing the government.

"One time, I didn't do well in my final exams in biology at university. My father was ready to take out his belt and hit me with it, but Doug snatched the belt from him and barked at him. It helped by postponing the punishment, but it did not eliminate it. I was hit later that day when my father locked Doug in one of the rooms."

"Doug sounds like the man," I say, trying to shift the conversation from her father.

"He was...I really miss him. He was there for me when even my brother wasn't," she scoffs, making my heart squeeze a little.

I take her hand in mine and squeeze a little, showing her that I am here for her. "Ana, look I don't want to defend Andrew, but he really cared for you and still does. He just wanted to protect you from all the mafia shit."

"Did he? Did he protect me? I would rather get mixed up with this mafia shit than get beaten by my father just because I was not as perfect as his real kids."

"You are right," I finally say, pulling her to my chest and hugging her.

Andrew is one of my best friends. We met in college back in the day, but I never knew a lot about his family. He took a bullet for me and I will forever trust him. I respected that he didn't want to tell us about his family. I wouldn't want to tell anyone about my family if mine was like his. His parents and other sister were crazy.

"Anyways, would you like to do something?" she asks, biting her lips and driving me crazy.

"Something like what?" I smirk, leaning close to her and looking at her cleavage.

"You pervert! Something like watching a movie," she replies, slapping my arm gently.

"You are no fun," I say with a pout.

"I know, but you still like me," she says.

"That you're right," I reply with a smile.

We sit on my bed and open my laptop. It is midnight and the only thing that I want to do at this moment is spending time with her.

"What do you want to watch?" I ask.

"Are you up for something like Pride and Prejudice?" she asks.

"I will watch anything you want to," I reply.

"Okay, thank you," she shyly replies.

I grab her chin and press my lips, stealing a quick kiss. "You should know that from now on, you are mine and I am yours, Si?"

She shyly looks down and nods, not trusting her words.

The movie starts and we cuddle together as we watch.

Waking up next to Ana and sleeping beside her, in general, was one of the best things I experienced. For the first time ever, I don't get nightmares of the day my father was taken by the police because of Ricardo.

"Good morning," I say as soon as I see her wake up.

"Good morning." She smiles, stretching her arm. "This is the best sleep ever."

"I was thinking the same," I reply with a grin.

"We should do it more often," she suggests, making me smirk.

"I agree."

After a few minutes, Ana walks to her room and I go to the bathroom to take a shower. I brush my teeth and wrap the black towel around my torso when I finish.

Walking back into my room, I take out my outfit for the day, which insists on a black shirt and navy pants with a matching jacket.

I have an important meeting today with old friends, Mia Gonzalez and River Martin. They have their own technology company, where they sell innovative products. But that is not the only thing they could do. Mia's father was the leader of the Spanish mafia in the past. When he retired, my father took over. Mia didn't want to become the Donna of her father's mafia, so she and her husband founded this company to help mafia families with hacking and finding information.

That is why I am meeting with them. I need them to find the person who killed Jao Gorden, who my father was accused of killing. Jao was a nurse at the hospital. My father was visiting Ricardo that day. My father saw someone killing Jao, but his face was hidden. The problem is that Ricardo threatened my father that if he opened his mouth and didn't take the blame, he will leak a video of me killing one of our enemies.

So, now we have to find two videos, the one where I killed that asshole, and the one that would get my father freedom.

I leave the house but not before kissing Ana. I drive to the meeting location, Mia's and River's farmhouse here in Cape Breton Island. We will need to move out of this island very soon because people started recognizing us and it is soon that the police would. We need to go to Mexico very soon, but it is very hard to travel without being noticed. The only thing that could work is if we traveled either by water, or private jet, which I don't have but need to buy.

I reach the destination and park my car near the entrance. The house looks vintage and doe a moment, I feel that I need one of those.

I knock on the door and wait for someone to open it. After two minutes, the door finally opens and an old woman stood behind it.

"Hello, sir, welcome," she politely greets, opening the door further for me to enter. She motions for me to follow her and I do. We walk through two hallways before standing in front of brown double doors. She knocks before opening the doors.

The room is a huge office. A desk stood on the left side of the room, while two huge couches sat across from it, to my right. Mia and Martin are sitting on the couch and as soon as they see me, they stand up and smile.

"Welcome, Rafael," River says, giving me a side hug.

"Hey, Rafael, long time no see." Mia smiles and hugs me.

"Hey, guys, long time no see indeed. How has it been?" I ask, sitting down across from them.

"Good. To much work between Canada and Spain. We haven't been here in months," Mia replies.

"I am glad you are here," I say.

"What is going on, Rafa? How is your father?" River asks.

I sigh. "He is good, but I need to clear his name and I need your help."

"Of course, with whatever you need," Mia replies.

"I need you to find me footage of the third floor, room 241, Vancouver hospital on June 13, 2021. My father was framed for a murder that night and he saw the murderer in that room."

"I will see what we can do, Rafa, don't worry," River says, making me feel slightly better. "I am sorry we couldn't help you out earlier, but we are here now."

"Don't worry about it, man. I understand."

Mia and River had gone through so much pain the past year. Mia and River lost their five-day-old son from heart complications. I remember visiting the funeral that day, but I couldn't stay for too long because I couldn't deal with it. It was too much.

"How are you feeling?" I ask them.

"Living..." Mia replies with a weak smile.

"We are trying again..." River announces, making me smile.

"That is great!" I say with a smile.

Mia smiles and looks at me. "So, is there a woman in your life, Rafa?" she wiggles her brows.

I roll my eyes playfully and confess. "You could say that," I reply shyly.

"Oh my god, what is her name?" Mia squeals excitedly.

"Ana."

"Wait, is she the doctor who took care of your father in prison?" River asks.

"How do you know that?"

"Alex told me when I spoke to him on the phone the other day. He said that your father offered her work."

"Yeah...and I still can't believe she agreed."

"I guess it is in her blood as well," Mia comments, making me nod with a smile.

"Couldn't agree more."

Chapter 24. Finding Truth pt. 2

Rafael

"I can't believe you found it," I say in disbelief as I look at the screen.

"It took about 5 hours without break to find it, but I finally did. It was hidden deep in the database as if someone made sure no one could find it," Mia replies with a triumphed look.

"No one but you, I guess," I reply with a grin.

Relief washes over knowing that I will finally free my father with this video. We tried so hard to find the video, but lost hope when we couldn't find anything about that night.

"How are we going to deliver it?" River asks.

"I feel it is best for Uncle Manuel to deliver it himself," Mia suggests.

5 Hours Earlier

I went back back and waited till Mia and River to find the video I was looking for.

I found Alba and Ana sitting together with Cash and Alex in the game room. The guys were playing FIFA, while the girls are talking and eating snacks. I could tell they were gossiping about the guys, mainly Cash.

Just a feeling.

"Hey," I said, making myself known.

"Hey," they all replied at the same time.

I sat beside Ana and wrapped one arm around her shoulder. "How are you?" I whispered to her ear.

She smiled and said, "Good, and you?"

"Good. I have missed you."

"Me too...you were gone for hours. Did you find the thing you were looking for?" she asks, her features turning serious.

"Soon. They are on it," I replied.

"How are Mia and River?" Alba asked sympathetically.

"They are still not okay, but doing their best and moving on. They are trying for a baby again."

"Really?!" Alba squealed, excited to finally hear that they are finally trying again.

"What happened with them, if you don't mind me asking?" Ana asked nervously.

"They lost their baby last year. It was a very hard time for them," I explained to Ana.

"Oh..." Ana mumbled, drifting to a past memory because she suddenly focused on the table in front of her and thought hard.

"Are you okay?" I asked, caressing her cheek.

She looked up at me and smiled weakly. "Yeah...I just remembered the day my parents adopted me. It was the happiest day of my life..."

"This is your family now, Ana. You should know that I, no we, love you so much," I said with a serious face.

"Thank you, Rafa." She pecks my lips, causing Alba to gasp.

"When the fuck did you both get together?" she yelled enough for the guys to hear. Cash turned around and said, "Now, you realized?"

"I didn't! I saw," she said.

"We kind of got together yesterday," Ana said shyly, tucking a strand of hair behind her ear.

"This is a scandal! This is...is...I am mad at you for not telling me!" Alba pointed at Ana.

"I was shy, Alba, you know me..."

Alba looked at her with narrowed eyes then at me, and said, "Fine, I'll let it go this time, but I swear if you get pregnant and I am not the first person you tell, I will kill you!"

"I, I would be the first one to know," I said with furrowed eyebrows.

Alba rolled her eyes and took her phone out.

I grabbed Ana's hand with mine and intertwined our fingers. I kept drawing circles in the palm of her hand, while I looked at her beautiful face.

"Why are you looking at me like that?" she asked with a grin.

"I can't get over how beautiful you are and I can't believe that we are together," I replied genuinely, feeling over the moon that she is mine.

"Don't say that here," she shyly said, looking at our intertwined fingers.

I chuckled and pulled her close to me. "I can't believe you are mine," I whispered this time, causing her cheeks to turn dark shades of red.

"By the way, Rafa," Cash spoke up, grabbing everyone's attention, including mine.

"Yeah, man?" I replied.

"I will be going for a few days," he said, making me cross my eyebrows in confusion.

Where would he go while the police were after him?

"Where?" Alba questions before I could open my mouth.

"Somewhere..." Cash replied, not giving her the answer she wanted, and there I knew that he was leaving because of her and this 'boyfriend' of hers. His eyes are so dull unlike before. His face is paler and he is not eating well. I would know because we only eat together.

I motioned for him to follow me and I walked to the far end of the room so no one could hear us.

I waited for him to come and when he did, I asked him what was wrong.

"Nothing, man. I just need to get away for a while."

"Are you feeling okay? I noticed you are not eating and clearly not sleeping well, and you only play FIFA whenever you want to get your mind off something, so what is it?"

"I-It's nothing, I promise."

"Is it because of Alba?" I whispered, making his eyes widen in shock.

"How the fuck do you all-" he mumbled, closing his eyes and letting out a heavy sigh. "W-What do you mean?"

I rolled my eyes and said, "You are too obvious, you know?"

"I will stop, are you mad?"

"I'd definitely prefer you over whoever she is dating..."

"I know...I want to kill him!" he replied with passion.

"So, you are okay with it?" he hesitantly asked.

"No, but as I said, I prefer you over anyone for that matter."

"Good because I am not giving up," he said with determination.

"Good. Now, promise me to take care of yourself. You look like shit," I pointed out.

"I promise."

As soon as our conversation ended, I got a call from Mia telling me to come fast to her home. She told me she found something and that it might be the video I was looking for.

I quickly hang up and told everyone that I am leaving. I told them not to say anything to my father because I didn't want to give false hopes. I wanted to surprise him and ensure that it is the right video to get him his freedom.

I stepped into my car and drove to Mia and River's house.

Present Time

"Are you sure that is what he should do?" I ask Mia, who suggested the idea of having my father deliver the video to the police on his own.

I did like the idea at first, but I am scared now a little bit because I don't want the video to fall to the wrong person at the station.

"How about we share the video with the whole country and make sure everyone knows that Manuel Santos is an innocent man?" I suggest.

"Smart idea. I don't know why I went with that one first," Mia replies, making River and I chuckle.

"Anyways, thank you so much, guys. I will never forget this. I owe you," I say gratefully.

"Don't thank us, Rafael. We are family," River replies with a nod.

"Thanks."

I tell Mia to put the video on a USB and keep a copy with her in case something happens. She also stored the video on many USBs and hard disks, just to be sure.

I drive back home and get excited to see my father and tell him about the news.

This video came in time because on my way back to the house, a police car stopped me and showed me a picture of my father, asking me if I saw this man. I have always found this way so inefficient because anyone could lie and it would help the criminal or the person running way from being caught.

When I reach the house, I park my car and run inside. Everyone is sitting in the living room when I walk in, which is the perfect time to tell the news to everyone.

"Dad," I call my father.

"Yeah, son?"

I take out the USB and show it to him.

"What is this?" he asks.

"I will show you," I say, getting the laptop from the next room and inserting the USB. I raise the volume and make sure everyone could see the video from where they are sitting.

As soon as the video started, everyone, especially my father, has his eyes widen in shock and disbelief at what he is watching. Even I, watching it again, feel that it is unbelievable. I knew that this video existed before, but it was impossible to find. Mia and River are so smart that they could find anything you want in a matter of hours. This video was hidden so well that only one person could have done that and that is Ricardo. Of course, he was the one behind the attack and the framing.

"Son, where did you get this?"

"Mia and River Gonzalez."

"This means..."

"Yes, father, it means that you will be a free man very soon."

Chapter 25. Tabloids: Manuel González is Innocent

Rafael

"I can't believe this," my father mumbles, his eyes not leaving the laptop's screen.

My mother is in shock, as well as, my siblings. Even Cassie and Ana could not believe that the video is live in front of them.

"The police need to see this as soon as possible," my mother points out.

"I will give it to the tabloids and post it on the internet. It is easier to spread the news that way. After that, I will send it to the officials," I explain. "I also made sure that Mia has so many copies in case something happens, but it will be out everywhere, so there will be no need for that."

My father stands up and walks my way. He hugs me and thanks me for finding the video. "Thank you, Rafa. I am so proud of you."

I smile and hug him back without saying anything. He knows how much his words mean to me, so there is no need.

"I will go take care of the video and will get back to you as soon as I am finished," I say, earning nods from everyone but Ana.

"I am coming with you," she says.

"You don't have to, mi amor," I reply.

"I insist," she replies.

Manuel

For a year and a half now, I have lived my life running away and locked up. I knew that this life, being a mafia boss, would have consequences but I did not expect them to come from my best friend, my brother.

I hadn't seen my family for a year and I will never forgive Ricardo for that. I will kill him myself and it won't be an easy death for him. I will torture him until he begs me to spare his life. But I wouldn't. I wouldn't spare his life and then postpone his death as much as I could, making him wish I end it quickly.

During my time at prison, I had dreamed of reuniting with my family. I did not know what I did wrong to get such a punishment and betrayal from Ricardo, but I knew later after searching through my mind in the lonely days that Ricardo liked my wife, Victoria. At first, I didn't question his intentions towards my wife whenever we got together for movie nights with our other friends. When he got to the point of being clingy, I still didn't question it but I put some boundaries for him. But when I was arrested after he set me up, I became sure that he liked Victoria and wanted her for himself, and what better way than to have me out of the way?

The good thing is, my wife and son discovered that he was the one behind the attack because I left a riddle for Rafa to solve when he sent someone to visit me. He couldn't come himself and I understand why. The last thing we want is for anyone to know I am married and have kids because I don't want them to get linked to me whenever anything happens. I trained Alba and Rafael so well to know how to act in these situations.

When I reunited with Victoria and my kids again, I felt like my soul came back into my body. The void that once lived inside disintegrated and life came back better than before.

Now hearing that my life could be the same as before and even better, makes me feel so thankful and grateful. I never doubted my son and I knew that one day he will clear my name to live a normal life even though the mafia is not normal.

"Mi amor, are you okay?" my gorgeous wife asks as she circles her arms around my back, resting her face in the crook of my neck.

"I am now," I reply with a smile, turning around to face her. Her arms are now wrapped around my waist as mine are around hers.

I take her hand in mine and walk to the balcony in our bedroom which has two chairs and a table in the middle. I pull the chair out for her and then sit on the one placed across from hers.

"Is there something bothering you?" she asks with a worried look.

"No, my love, just wanted to talk about Rafael."

"What about him?"

"I wanted to ask you if he told you anything about being serious with Ana. It is not that I don't trust him, in fact, I trust him blindly, but Ana is so precious to me and I don't want her to get hurt. She deserves the world just like Rafa."

She smiles warmly at me and says, "He didn't tell me anything, but I know he is so serious about her. He cares for her a lot and she does too. They just got together, mi amor, so it is early to talk about serious stuff like marriage and such, but I know Rafael. He is ready whether he realizes it or not."

"You are right, it is still early. I just want them to be happy, you know?" I scratch the back of my neck nervously.

"I know, my love. I do too. How about you talk to him? I am sure he will appreciate you talking to him," she suggests, making my heart leap. I can't talk to him, could I? I would just get nervous and awkward about it. I was never someone who knew how to talk about his feelings with his children. I only do that with my wife because she is my soulmate. But still, my children are very important to me and I would do anything for them, even if I have to talk about emotions and feelings with my son.

"You are right, mi flor. I will try talking to him."

She smiles and takes my hand in hers above the table. "I know it is hard for you and well, awkward, but you can do it. Besides,

I have had a lot of those with Alba and it wasn't fun at first, but trust me, it gets easier," she explains, making me chuckle.

"There is Alba too and that guy she is seeing. Did you manage to find out who?" I ask, narrowing my eyes at my precious wife.

"That's classified, but rest assured, he is clean."

"Is he nice to her?" I ask.

"Till now, yes, but he is still under trial. Besides, I didn't like him at first and I still don't. But let us see, our daughter likes him very much and in the two times I have seen him, he seems like he does too."

"Good because if he hurts her, I will bury him alive," I threaten, pointing my hand to nowhere in particular.

"Oh, honey, I would burn him alive, don't you worry."

"Good."

After a few hours of talking and flirting with one another, one of the maids brought us two newspapers and an iPad.

I was a little confused as to why she brought them, but after I glanced at the screen of the iPad, I understood.

Headlines: Manuel Santos is Innocent."A recent video surfaced of the allegedly Mafia Boss, Manuel Santos, the leader of De Santos Mafia, that shows the falsely accused being framed for a murder he did not commit. The video shows a masked man whose height and weight are different than the accused, while the accused stands in front of him as the man killed the nurse.

Police records show Manuel Santos' testimony claiming that "a masked man shot the nurse and pinned the blame on me." His testimony was not taken into consideration back then but after the video surfaced, the station of Vancouver puts out the statement that Manuel Santos is innocent and is granted his freedom. They will also compensate him for false imprisonment.

The department of justice is working hard to find the real criminal. In the meantime, the department sends its apologies to Manuel Santos and to the city that they have failed, letting a criminal roam free around the city and imprisoning an innocent man.

I look up at my wife's tearful eyes and smile weakly. "You are free, Manuel."

"I am, mi amor, I am free," I reply, a few tears betraying me and escaping my eyes.

She gets out of her seat and comes my way, sitting on my lap. She takes my face in her hands and smiles warmly. Her sparkly eyes awaken the butterflies resting in my stomach"I am so proud of you, Manuel. I can't believe that this nightmare is over."

"Me too, my love. I can't believe it," I reply, placing my hands around her neck, gently.

"I love you so much, Mannie."

"I love you too, my Vicky."

Chapter 26. Celebrations & A Tragedy

Ana

We have been celebrating since yesterday. The news of Manuel's innocence shocked the entire city and he finally could go out freely.

On the other hand, cash, Alex, and I will never get freedom. At least, that is what I believe. Cash and Alex are still wanted for escaping and I am still wanted for helping them. Yes, technically they escaped with Manuel, which makes him an aider, but is there proof that he told them to escape? Or that they know each other? No.

"Cheers to a new beginning!" Victoria holds her glass of juice up as she does not drink alcohol anymore. No one does in this house anymore. Like Victoria said, 'Alcohol is the cause of unhappiness.'

That is her opinion and everyone has the right to have one. I agree with her too. Everyone in this house does.

We raise our glasses and then drink. I know it is not a new beginning for anyone because we still have an enemy to chase, Ricardo, but still. For now, we don't have to deal with him since he is in Italy, but I feel that he is going to come to Spain very soon and that is when Rafa and the rest will capture him.

Don't chase the enemy, wait till they come to you.

And Ricardo will come to us.

"We need to go somewhere and celebrate," Alba says, making me and the brothers to frown.

"They are still under the radar," Rafa replies for us.

"Well, it is easy to go undercover. We have always done it," she replies with a shrug.

"Okay, but we can't do it now. All eyes will be on me," Uncle replies, earning nods from everyone around the room.

"You are right, honey. We can always do that later. Let us just celebrate here tonight," Victoria says with a warm smile, trying to please everyone, especially her daughter.

Rafael

I take Alex and Cash on the side, not wanting to ruin the celebration vibes in the living room with work.

The three of us have been trying to find Ricardo's exact location because I am planning to finally take him out. But I need to plan it very well before doing anything because I will not just sit here and wait for him to come to Spain. He is a coward, someone who will never show his face in front of us, not since my father is back. At least, that is what I hope he is.

"Any news?" I ask, looking at both of them.

Alex speaks first. "From the data I last collected, he is still in Italy."

"We will keep looking, man, don't worry," Cash assures me, patting my shoulder.

"We have to. I can't live like this knowing that he is still out there. I have given him a free pass for almost two years and it is not going to go any longer."

"You are right. We will make sure he is captured soon," Alex replies with a nod.

We go back to the living room and I join my girlfriend, wrapping my right arm around her shoulder and giving her a million's dollar smile. She smiles back at me and pecks my lips quickly, so no one notices.

Suddenly, the door bell rings and Cash gets up to open. After a minute or so, Andrew walks in behind Cash to the living room.

"Hello, honey!" my mother hugs Andrew, making me feel utterly jealous. I narrow my eyes at her and she smiles sheepishly at me.

"I love you, honey," she mouths at me, making me smile.

Andrew hugs everyone and when he reaches Ana, they awkwardly hug fast and he sits next to her on the other side.

"Congratulations, uncle," Andrew says to my father.

"Thanks, son. I am glad it is over," my father replies with a smile. "Those three are still wanted, though. We have to do something about it," he continues, pointing at Ana, Cash, and Alex.

"I will try to find a way to get them out of this," Andrew says.

"You...don't have to do anything. I will figure it out," Ana stubbornly says. "Besides, father is still missing, so you can take care about that."

"It is okay, I want to do it," he replies with a shrug and then stills as he looks at everyone.

"What is it?" I ask, furrowing my eyebrows at his sudden change in mood.

"I don't mean to ruin the mood, but...I just received a call that they found father's body."

"What?!" All of us yell.

"Why haven't the news talked about it?" Ana asks.

"I just received the call. I am sure if you opened the TV, they will have something about that," Andrew replies, pointing at the TV.

I open the TV and surely, Benjamin's face is on the screen, announced dead this evening.

What is bothering me is that they are saying good things about him.

"Great, now they will blame me for his murder," Ana mutters angrily.

I raise the volume and the reporter reveals the cause of death.

"The FBI this evening found the body of Benjamin Wright, a famous surgeon and politician. He has been found in one of his properties he bought over the years with his wife in Mexico, dead. The cause of death is heart attack."

"I guess not," Ana continues.

"Thank god, we didn't move to Mexico," Victoria points out.

"I know! I guess karma is real," Ana replies, looking at the picture of her father that she clearly hates on the screen.

"You should check up on your mother and sister. I am sure they need you now," Ana tells Andrew, who avoids looking at her eyes.

I kind of feel bad for him. I know how much he loves Ana, but at the same time, I understand why she can't let herself forgive him.

"I would rather be here...with you," Andrew replies with a weak smile.

"Oh my god! Really? That is so nice of you," Ana dramatically and fake squeals.

She suddenly feels that she had taken it too far and frowns. She looks between everyone, who are already looking at her and says, "I think we should talk."

Andrew nods and the two of them go somewhere inside to talk.

"I hope they solve their problem because it is getting out of hand," Alba comments.

"If I did that to you, would you forgive me?" I ask her.

She glares and me and says, "No." She huffs and continues. "You are right. I would actually kill you."

I swallow hard because everyone and I mean everyone hates Alba's glary eyes, even love-sick puppy, Cash.

Before anyone could say anything else, the door bell rings again, making us all confused.

"Who could it be?" I ask, standing up to open it when all of a sudden, the entire house shakes and the sound of a bomb going off almost tear my ear.

I place my hands on my ear, trying to block the sound out, but it was too loud.

I saw fire everywhere and the only thought in my head is my family and girl friend who is somewhere with her brother.

I suddenly feel dizzy and the last thing I saw was looking at everyone's unconscious bodies on the floor.

The buzzing in my ears wakes me up. I could not adjust to my surroundings at first, but when I pulled my body up, I gain conscious. I look up at Andrew, who is holding Ana's unconscious body in his arms as he tries to wake me up. I see the fire cooled out and frown in confusion as to how that happened.

"We were inside talking when we felt it. I was the first one to wake up and quickly came here, putting the fire out," Andrew explains, pointing with his eyes at the fire extinguisher. "I then went back to Ana and came back here. She is not waking up, Rafa, please help her," he pleads, placing her on the corner on the floor.

I quickly take a look at her and sigh in relief when I felt her breathing. "She is okay, she will wake up soon."

I look around the living room with Andrew and try to wake everyone up.

As I look around, I notice that my mother is not here, neither is Alex.

I look at Andrew with wide eyes.

"It can't be..." I mumble.

"Calm down, I am sure they woke up before us and went to call for help."

"What help?! Alex is wanted by the police!" I exclaim.

"Oh my god...we have to clear this place as soon as possible!" I yell.

Andrew got the car ready while I woke everyone up. Thank god no one has major injuries. It was like someone did this on purpose, not wanting to kill us.

"Where is Victoria?" My father asks weakly, barely opening his eyes.

"Dad, we need to get you to the car, now."

"Where is your mother, Rafa?" he asks more firmly now.

"I don't know. She and Alex are gone," I reply, looking at Cash who has a dumbstruck look on his face.

Chapter 27. Victoria Santos

Ana

We have been celebrating since yesterday. The news of Manuel's innocence shocked the entire city and he finally could go out freely.

On the other hand, cash, Alex, and I will never get freedom. At least, that is what I believe. Cash and Alex are still wanted for escaping and I am still wanted for helping them. Yes, technically they escaped with Manuel, which makes him an aider, but is there proof that he told them to escape? Or that they know each other? No.

"Cheers to a new beginning!" Victoria holds her glass of juice up as she does not drink alcohol anymore. No one does in this house anymore. Like Victoria said, 'Alcohol is the cause of unhappiness.'

That is her opinion and everyone has the right to have one. I agree with her too. Everyone in this house does.

We raise our glasses and then drink. I know it is not a new beginning for anyone because we still have an enemy to chase, Ricardo, but still. For now, we don't have to deal with him since he is in Italy, but I feel that he is going to come to Spain very soon and that is when Rafa and the rest will capture him.

Don't chase the enemy, wait till they come to you.

And Ricardo will come to us.

"We need to go somewhere and celebrate," Alba says, making me and the brothers to frown.

"They are still under the radar," Rafa replies for us.

"Well, it is easy to go undercover. We have always done it," she replies with a shrug.

"Okay, but we can't do it now. All eyes will be on me," Uncle replies, earning nods from everyone around the room.

"You are right, honey. We can always do that later. Let us just celebrate here tonight," Victoria says with a warm smile, trying to please everyone, especially her daughter.

Rafael

I take Alex and Cash on the side, not wanting to ruin the celebration vibes in the living room with work.

The three of us have been trying to find Ricardo's exact location because I am planning to finally take him out. But I need to plan it very well before doing anything because I will not just sit here and wait for him to come to Spain. He is a coward, someone who will never show his face in front of us, not since my father is back. At least, that is what I hope he is.

"Any news?" I ask, looking at both of them.

Alex speaks first. "From the data I last collected, he is still in Italy."

"We will keep looking, man, don't worry," Cash assures me, patting my shoulder.

"We have to. I can't live like this knowing that he is still out there. I have given him a free pass for almost two years and it is not going to go any longer."

"You are right. We will make sure he is captured soon," Alex replies with a nod.

We go back to the living room and I join my girlfriend, wrapping my right arm around her shoulder and giving her a million's dollar smile. She smiles back at me and pecks my lips quickly, so no one notices.

Suddenly, the door bell rings and Cash gets up to open. After a minute or so, Andrew walks in behind Cash to the living room.

"Hello, honey!" my mother hugs Andrew, making me feel utterly jealous. I narrow my eyes at her and she smiles sheepishly at me.

"I love you, honey," she mouths at me, making me smile.

Andrew hugs everyone and when he reaches Ana, they awkwardly hug fast and he sits next to her on the other side.

"Congratulations, uncle," Andrew says to my father.

"Thanks, son. I am glad it is over," my father replies with a smile. "Those three are still wanted, though. We have to do something about it," he continues, pointing at Ana, Cash, and Alex.

"I will try to find a way to get them out of this," Andrew says.

"You...don't have to do anything. I will figure it out," Ana stubbornly says. "Besides, father is still missing, so you can take care about that."

"It is okay, I want to do it," he replies with a shrug and then stills as he looks at everyone.

"What is it?" I ask, furrowing my eyebrows at his sudden change in mood.

"I don't mean to ruin the mood, but...I just received a call that they found father's body."

"What?!" All of us yell.

"Why haven't the news talked about it?" Ana asks.

"I just received the call. I am sure if you opened the TV, they will have something about that," Andrew replies, pointing at the TV.

I open the TV and surely, Benjamin's face is on the screen, announced dead this evening.

What is bothering me is that they are saying good things about him.

"Great, now they will blame me for his murder," Ana mutters angrily.

I raise the volume and the reporter reveals the cause of death.

"The FBI this evening found the body of Benjamin Wright, a famous surgeon and politician. He has been found in one of his properties he bought over the years with his wife in Mexico, dead. The cause of death is heart attack."

"I guess not," Ana continues.

"Thank god, we didn't move to Mexico," Victoria points out.

"I know! I guess karma is real," Ana replies, looking at the picture of her father that she clearly hates on the screen.

"You should check up on your mother and sister. I am sure they need you now," Ana tells Andrew, who avoids looking at her eyes.

I kind of feel bad for him. I know how much he loves Ana, but at the same time, I understand why she can't let herself forgive him.

"I would rather be here...with you," Andrew replies with a weak smile.

"Oh my god! Really? That is so nice of you," Ana dramatically and fake squeals.

She suddenly feels that she had taken it too far and frowns. She looks between everyone, who are already looking at her and says, "I think we should talk."

Andrew nods and the two of them go somewhere inside to talk.

"I hope they solve their problem because it is getting out of hand," Alba comments.

"If I did that to you, would you forgive me?" I ask her.

She glares and me and says, "No." She huffs and continues. "You are right. I would actually kill you."

I swallow hard because everyone and I mean everyone hates Alba's glary eyes, even love-sick puppy, Cash.

Before anyone could say anything else, the door bell rings again, making us all confused.

"Who could it be?" I ask, standing up to open it when all of a sudden, the entire house shakes and the sound of a bomb going off almost tear my ear.

I place my hands on my ear, trying to block the sound out, but it was too loud.

I saw fire everywhere and the only thought in my head is my family and girl friend who is somewhere with her brother.

I suddenly feel dizzy and the last thing I saw was looking at everyone's unconscious bodies on the floor.

The buzzing in my ears wakes me up. I could not adjust to my surroundings at first, but when I pulled my body up, I gain conscious. I look up at Andrew, who is holding Ana's unconscious body in his arms as he tries to wake me up. I see the fire cooled out and frown in confusion as to how that happened.

"We were inside talking when we felt it. I was the first one to wake up and quickly came here, putting the fire out," Andrew explains, pointing with his eyes at the fire extinguisher. "I then went back to Ana and came back here. She is not waking up, Rafa, please help her," he pleads, placing her on the corner on the floor.

I quickly take a look at her and sigh in relief when I felt her breathing. "She is okay, she will wake up soon."

I look around the living room with Andrew and try to wake everyone up.

As I look around, I notice that my mother is not here, neither is Alex.

I look at Andrew with wide eyes.

"It can't be..." I mumble.

"Calm down, I am sure they woke up before us and went to call for help."

"What help?! Alex is wanted by the police!" I exclaim.

"Oh my god...we have to clear this place as soon as possible!" I yell.

Andrew got the car ready while I woke everyone up. Thank god no one has major injuries. It was like someone did this on purpose, not wanting to kill us.

"Where is Victoria?" My father asks weakly, barely opening his eyes.

"Dad, we need to get you to the car, now."

"Where is your mother, Rafa?" he asks more firmly now.

"I don't know. She and Alex are gone," I reply, looking at Cash who has a dumbstruck look on his face.

Chapter 28. An Old Friend

Ana

"I want to come with you," I announce making him turn 180 degrees to look at me.

"It is dangerous, Ana. I can't let you come," Rafael replies, grabbing two pistols and placing them behind his back.

"Please, Rafa, I can't let you go alone."

"I am not going alone, Ana."

"I know but-"

"Enough!" he yells, making me take a step back from his sudden outburst.

Rafael never yelled at me before. Not once. I understand that he is nervous and scared because he doesn't know his mother's condition, but I did not expect him to yell at me.

"Fine..." my voice dies down.

His eyes soften for a bit, knowing very well that he shouldn't have yelled, but he doesn't comment any further. He even left without telling me anything else as if I was the one who kidnapped his mother.

What the fuck has gotten into him?

I climb the stairs from the basement back to the living room, only to see Cash and Manuel ready to take off to the warehouse. Manuel finally talked to Cash this morning and uncle understood that Cash had nothing to do with what his brother did.

"Uncle..." I call after him.

He turns and looks at me with a weak smile. "Take care and bring her back," I say.

"I will and you take care, mi hija. Don't leave the house at all. There will be guards here with you and Alba, and Rafael told Cody to come here as well."

"Okay..." I give him a nod.

"Now let us hope we find her location," Manuel mumbles, making my heart clench.

I hope so too.

Rafael

I walk to my car without looking back because I know that it will not be easy to let her go if I do. After what happened to my father when my mother was kidnapped, I don't ever want to love again. What if something happens to Ana because of my work and she gets kidnapped, or worse, killed? I can't live with that. I can't put her in danger and when I come back from this mission, the first thing I am going to do is send her away.

I know she is still wanted by the police, but I will make sure to clear her name and let her go.

I know...I am selfish, I admit, but put yourself in my shoes, what would you have done? Would you put the person you love in danger?

Cash hops into the passenger seat while we wait for my father. He looks at me and I could feel his gaze from the corner of my right eye, but I pay him no attention. I know exactly what is going on in his mind and I don't wish to talk about it.

My father then joins us and steps into the backseat. Driving off to the warehouse, I look in the rearview mirror to see Alba and Ana standing outside, looking our way.

I feel bad. So bad. But it took me a night to think about everything and take the decision. She still doesn't know but she will when I come back and tell her. Right now, all I am thinking about is finding my mother.

"How will we find her?" my father asks.

"Luckily, I learned a thing or two from Alex's hacking skills. I will try to find her, father, but I need the right equipment."

"Tell me whatever you need and we will get it," I reply.

"Well, just a good network I guess," Cash replies with a shrug.

I roll my eyes playfully as I park the car in front of the new building. We have moved the warehouse so many times, just because our enemies are finding its location.

We walk in and see Andrew standing by the gate, waiting for us.

"Any news?" I ask him as we all walk to the basement.

"No," he replies.

We walk to the basement and Cash immediately got the laptop and starts working.

From what I understood, he has to find footage of the car they took my mother in. Luckily, we have cameras close to the house we were staying at.

"Okay, here's the car leaving the house," Cash says, making us all look at the screen. "But the footage stops at this road, which has two ways. If they went right, they would have gone to the neighboring, but if they went left, they would have gone to the ports," Cash explains.

"Is Ricardo stupid enough to take my mother to the neighboring town, knowing very well that it would be easy to find them?" Andrew asks.

"No," I reply to him.

"This means, he went to the ports because there is a way to reach Italy by ship," my father says.

"I don't care if he is in Italy, we are going," I say firmly.

"Okay, I will check if there are any cameras at the ports." Cash quickly types on the keyboard.

Andrew, my father, and I wait impatiently for Cash until he finally yells the 'I found it.'

"What did you find?" I ask, running to his side and clutching the back of the back as I look at the screen.

"Look here," he says, pointing at an area on the screen. "This is the same car that left the house with your mother in it. In this next footage-" he presses the right arrow, taking us to the next footage, "-you can see the men loading something onto the boat. The camera is not focusing on it, but I am sure it is your mother."

"Is there a way we can know where the boat went?" My father asks.

"Unfortunately, no, but what I know is that the closest port to us is Pisa's, but we have Nice of France closer."

"Ricardo is banned from going to France," my father says, dismissing the idea of his former best friend going to France.

"But he can go in illegally, no?" Andrew asks.

"I doubt he'd go there, especially while kidnapping a person. He hasn't visited France in a very long time, so I doubt him going there. Italy is the safest place for him, especially since he knows we have little men to none there."

"Well, I guess it is time to call an old friend," my father says with a sigh.

"And who is that?" I ask, confused as to who my father knows in Italy.

"Your mother's old friend, Amalia Ferrari."

Chapter 29. Rescuing Victoria Santos

Rafael

It took us a whole day to reach Italy by sea, and another day to find Amalia Ferrari, who turned out to be very hard to find and an impossible person to talk to. Her guards had to be put down (not dead) in order for us to enter her house. We didn't have her phone number and trust me, we tried to find it illegally but this woman was untraceable.

We were standing in front of her huge villa in Sicily, admiring the house and writing down notes to redecorate our house.

We knocked on the huge double doors and waited for some-one to open them, hoping someone was inside. As much as

I was willing to barge inside, I didn't want to disrespect her further, especially when I don't know how she is.

After two minutes, the door opened and a young girl stood behind it. She looked to be ten years old and had blonde hair brighter than the sun.

"MAMA!" she yelled once she didn't recognize us, running back inside and leaving the door open.

An older woman appeared from inside with the young girl trailing behind her. The woman looked at me first then at my father. Cash stood behind us but she didn't spare him a look.

"Took you too long," she said, looking at my father.

"You knew we were coming?" I asked in confusion, making her look at me.

"Of course, I knew. Once I heard your mother was missing, I knew your father would come," she explained, ushering us in, but not before looking back at the entrance where the unconscious bodies of the guards laid.

But she didn't say anything as if she knew that would happen.

She took us to the living room and there, we saw a man who looked like the young girl, sitting on the sofa reading a newspaper.

"Welcome," he simply said, earning a nod from us.

"So? Tell me, what do you want?" Amalia asked my father.

"We need your help in finding Victoria," my father replied.

"I know, but what do you need? Weapons? Men?"

"Both...and hopefully, your husband," my father said, glancing at the man sitting.

"Me? Why?" the man asked in confusion.

"You were in the military and used to be Amalia's bodyguard."

"I am still is," the man replied, smiling at his wife.

"Anyways, we know that Ricardo took her to Sicily, so they must be here somewhere. Could you ask around people you trust?" I asked her.

"I don't trust anyone," she replied with a firm look on her face. "If we are going to find her, we will have to do it ourselves."

"How?" My father asked.

"We'll break down every door if we have to."

Amalia insisted we stay at her house. She told us that her husband, Alessandro, was going to get us more men to come with us on the mission. He also said that there are three places

Ricardo could be at. One, the ports, two, the old and abandoned sewing factory, and third, an underground facility, one that could only be in the heart of the city.

So the next day, we all got ready. Amalia's daughter, Lily, was sent to her grandmother in France, while we left the villa and started our search.

We split into two groups so we don't draw attention to ourselves. For all we knew, Ricardo already knew that we were in Sicily, but I had hoped that he didn't.

We first searched for places that could lead to underground facilities. We went to the heart of the city and asked a bit around, but made sure not to directly ask someone. We blended in with the people and I thanked my mother that she taught us Italian when we were younger because she knew that one day we will need it. Besides, Ricardo used to speak Italian with us to "help" my mother teach us the language.

When we didn't find anywhere that would lead underground, we then went to the ports. Since they traveled by sea, they had to enter Sicily by boat, so Ricardo might have had a place at the ports. but I highly doubted that. It was too open and anyone could find him there.

"They are not here either," Alessandro said when we finished looking around the port.

"We still have one place to go before we look at other places," I said, feeling disappointed that we didn't find them.

"Don't worry, we will find your mother," Amalia said, patting my shoulder.

When we reached the old sewing factory, we split again into two groups. My father this time went with Amalia and Alessandro after I insisted because I knew Alessandro could protect him after what I learned about him, and Cash and I stayed together.

They went to the right and we went to the left. We saw one man standing outside the side door, guarding, and we instantly knew that they were there. The guard had a tattoo of a snake, which told me that he was one of Ricardo's men. Ricardo was obsessed with snakes as pets.

"How do you want to do it?" Cash asked in a whisper. We were hiding behind a car that was parked close to the side door where the man was standing.

"You go up and ask him about Alex and tell him that you are his brother. Then, surprise him with a punch?" I suggested, unsure of my plan.

I saw hurt pass through his eyes, but it quickly went away.

"Okay, I just hope there isn't anyone standing on the inside close to the door because it is weird they are putting only one person outside."

"Me too, but I think he didn't want to draw attention. Besides, Ricardo may be smart, but he makes a lot of mistakes," I replied, earning a nod.

With that, Cash took off and once the guard saw him, he quickly took out his gun, but Cash immediately said Alex's name and mentioned he was his brother. Once Cash stood close to him, he smacked the guard and he fell unconscious.

I then followed him and we carefully opened the door to check if there was anyone, but thankfully, there was not.

We walked in with guns in our hands, ready to shoot anyone that comes in our way. But before we could encounter anyone, we heard gunshots and we immediately knew that they saw the rest on the other side.

For the first time, my heart was beating so fast, scared that something bad happened to my father. He was not that old and still got the hang of everything, but still, after what happened with my mother, I get worried about everything.

"Don't worry, Amalia and Alessandro are with him. Let's find your mother," Cash whispered, making me refocus on the mission.

The action seemed to be on the other side of the factory, which was good for us. Cash and I found a staircase that took us to the first floor and there, we found five men standing, waiting for us as if they knew someone was coming.

Gunshots were fired and we immediately took refuge behind the wall. I started shooting in their direction, hitting one man in the stomach.

Cash took the other two, leaving three alive. They kept shooting until they ran out of bullets. While getting more, I quickly came out of hiding and shot them all.

At that time, Amalia, Alessandro, and my father came up the stairs and joined us.

"We searched the other side and we didn't find anything," Amalia said.

"They must be here, then," my father said, pointing at the door at the end of the corridor.

We carefully walked to the door, looking behind every time to make sure no one came.

I slowly opened the door and a bedroom greeted us. We looked ahead only to see Ricardo holding my mother's neck close to the window, ready to push her down.

"Rafa! Mannie!" my mother yelled as tears ran down her face.

"Leave her the fuck alone!" I yelled, pointing my gun at the fucker.

"I am impressed you found me," Ricardo said with an evil smirk. "But I am glad too because I want you to watch your precious little wife dead."

He was going to push her, but a gunshot from outside hit Ricardo in the head, letting his body fall to the ground.

I quickly ran to my mother and took her in my arms and away from the window. Cash looked outside only to see a helicopter in the sky with Alba hanging down with a rope and a sniper in her hand.

Needed to be steady my ass.

"Damn..." he mumbled, amazed by the image of his crush in the sky.

"You're safe..." I told my mother as I caressed her hair.

Chapter 30. Confrontation

Ana

Everything happened so fast. We were ordered to stay home surrounded by so many guards while the rest left on the mission to Italy. At first, Alba and I got defeated because we couldn't help, but then Alba came up with the craziest idea. She told me that she had a friend who had a boat that could get us to Italy without anyone detecting us.

"What about the guards?" I had asked her.

"Don't worry about them. I will make them leave," she had replied.

I didn't question her as long as she would take me with her to Italy. I hadn't anticipated that she would take one of the guns in the basement, shoot a guard in his leg and threaten the rest to kill him if they didn't leave. When a few guards ran her way to fight with her, they underestimated her. She kicked the one she was holding in the head till he fell unconscious, and fought with the rest, using the training her father taught her at a young age.

What I didn't think would happen was that she would take them all by herself, showing that these guards were useless.

She contacted her friend, and told us to meet him at the port, and took us to Italy. From there, Alba started looking for this woman, Amalia Ferrari. We surprisingly found her easily, only because we looked into surveillance forcefully. We found Rafa and the rest in one of the footage and we went to the location.

Unfortunately, we didn't find anyone at home, only guards, who were ready to shoot us, but didn't once we told them who we were. Amalia had a helicopter parked on the roof of her mansion, which we took forcefully as well.

There was only one problem.

We didn't know where they were.

But Alba solved that quickly.

"Did you plan on coming here?" I asked her, surprised to see a tracking device in her hand.

"I planned all along because I knew they wouldn't take me with them. They think I am still young, idiots."

That is how we knew their location and flew to it. I wasn't really prepared to witness Alba shooting someone's head with a sniper from the helicopter, but that is a story for another day.

A day later, we are back in Canada. Amalia insisted that we stay at her house for a few days, but Victoria wanted to return to heal from the traumatizing experience he just had.

Victoria stayed in her room with Manuel and didn't want to come out for a while. Thankfully, Manuel told us that Ricardo didn't do anything to her.

I was in Alba's room when she asked me about Rafael.

"So, what is going on with you and Rafa? We have been back here for two days and he hasn't been around much."

I sighed, knowing that I can't run away from this.

"I honestly don't know..." I replied. "He started acting weird ever since your mom was kidnapped and didn't talk to me about it again."

She shook her head as if she knew he would do that. "Of course, he would do that."

"What do you mean?" I asked.

She replied while putting her mascara on. "Well, he is scared that he is going to lose you. You are his weakness."

Oh.

"So he would just ghost me like that as if nothing happened?"

"Typical Rafael's behavior. He always detaches when something scares him. He gets scared because he thinks he can't protect you."

"I didn't know that he felt that way," I replied with a frown.

That meant that I didn't know Rafael that well, but I kind of understood him because it is not easy to deal with these emotions. I just wished he talked to me about it.

"Do you think I should talk to him?" I asked.

She sighed before turning to face me. "Yes. He needs reassurance."

"Okay..."

I went to Rafael's room and knocked on the door. When I didn't hear anything, I pushed the door open only to find him asleep. He looked so peaceful in his sleep that I wanted to caress his hair all night. His brown hair looked so soft. I didn't want to disturb him, so I switched off the lights because they were on, and turned out to leave.

"Ana?" His sleepy voice called, making me face him again.

"Sorry...I didn't mean to wake you up," I replied, getting nervous.

"It is fine. Did something happen?" he asked.

"No...no, nothing happened. I just...I just wanted to speak with you."

"Sure, come." He patted the mattress in front of him.

I closed the door and switched the lights on again. I sat in front of him on the bed and started fidgeting with my fingers as if we aren't a couple...or weren't?

"Tell me."

"I just...I know it is basically not the time after what happened, but can we talk about us?"

He sighed and covered his face with his hands, but didn't say anything.

"If you are scared that something might happen to me because of your job, don't. Nothing will happen to me because you will always be beside me."

His eyes met mine as if I just caught him in the act. "Did Alba tell you this?" he asked.

"Don't change the subject, Rafa."

"Fine...I am scared, yes. You don't understand, Ana. What happened to my mom...I can't live that again."

"So what? You just give up because something might happen to me? You can't do that, Rafa. The thing is...even if we break ...up...I will stay in this house. It is the same thing."

"You're right...I am sorry, Ana," he replied.

"Look," I started as a tear fell down hitting my cheeks. "I don't want to force you. If you don't want to be with me...I would understand."

"Don't say that, please," he replied, taking one hand in his while the other wiped the tears away.

Milton Keynes UK
Ingram Content Group UK Ltd.
UKHW021034111124
451035UK00017B/1287

9 798330 529117